BUILDING A COM[...]
WRITERS
Scripted Mini-lessons to Model the Craft of Writing

MW01274319

Written by
Kim Cernek

Editor: Collene Dobelmann
Illustrator: Jane Yamada
Designer/Production: Moonhee Pak/Carlie Hayashi
Cover Designer: Barbara Peterson
Art Director: Moonhee Pak
Project Director: Betsy Morris

Table of Contents

Unit 1: A Community of Writers

MINI-LESSONS

Unit 2: The Basics of Our Craft

MINI-LESSONS

Unit 3: Getting Started

MINI-LESSONS

Unit 4: Learning About Conventions

MINI-LESSONS

Introduction

Building a Community of Writers provides children in first and second grade with the tools and practices that enable them to become successful writers. The principles of Writer's Workshop are skillfully incorporated into 8 writing units that include scripted mini-lessons based on familiar literature. The guided activities of this systematic approach allow young writers to express their ideas fluently and with confidence.

A successful Writer's Workshop includes modeling the writing process for children. It guides children in planning and revising their stories. Writer's Workshop also includes the essential elements of writing conferences, direct instruction on grammar and mechanics, and opportunities to share.

At a glance, each **Writing Unit** consists of the following:

- **Four scripted mini-lessons** that incorporate the elements of Writer's Workshop to give children an awareness of good writing practices

- **Eight standards-based activities** that encourage students to practice what they've learned

- **A school-to-home** family letter and writing connection that helps parents support their children's development as writers

Methods of assessment and useful implementation strategies are also included as part of the field-tested lessons and activities in *Building a Community of Writers*.

This book provides the materials and motivation to establish a community of writers in your classroom. Using the dialogue outlined in the scripted lessons will help you introduce young learners to the idea that they are valued writers. **Note: the suggested script for what you might say is printed in blue ink each time a new skill is presented.** The children will inspire you to explore new avenues of writing with them, and they will ask for more time to write and share their work!

> Empower children to express themselves fluently and independently.

Writer's Workshop

Expose Children to Models of Good Writing

When exposed to models of good writing, children learn to experiment with new techniques, vocabulary, and writing styles. In each of the literature-based mini-lessons included in this book, there are two sections that encourage awareness and practice of good writing skills.

The "READ and THINK" part of each scripted mini-lesson shows children that we can learn how to be good writers by examining and discussing what good writers do. This section of each mini-lesson introduces and explores one or two elements of good writing. See page 96 for a complete list of the literature selections referenced in this book.

Invite Children to Apply What They Learn

The "WRITE and APPLY" part of each scripted mini-lesson invites children to implement what they've learned about effective writing in their own writing. This invitation to apply what they've learned about the elements of good writing encourages children to develop into independent writers.

The follow-up activities (labeled Activity A and Activity B) offer structured opportunities for children to use what they've learned in the scripted mini-lessons while practicing the skills that meet grade-level-appropriate literacy standards and benchmarks. The Standards Connection at the end of each lesson identifies the standards addressed.

Value Developmentally Appropriate Writing

By valuing children's developmentally appropriate writing, they will be esteemed and motivated to strive for continued progress as writers. It's important for children to understand that everyone in class is a writer.

Explain to children that writing is about communicating and sharing ideas with others. Point out that some beginning writers use pictures to write, some use letters, and others use words. Encourage children who are writing with illustrations to write the first sound of the object in their illustration.

> Explain to children that some beginning writers use pictures to write, some use letters, and others use words.

Guide children who use invented spelling toward using conventional spelling. Note that Writer's Workshop is not the time to correct conventions (i.e., spelling, grammar, punctuation) rather, it is the time to encourage children to explore how these conventions are used in context.

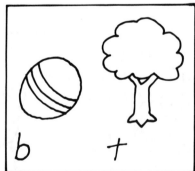

Give Children an Audience

Young writers must have the opportunity to share their work with their writing community. Knowing they will have an audience, they will be more interested in producing quality writing. The audience will benefit by hearing a variety of writings and by practicing their active listening skills.

Sharing at School

Reserve the last few minutes of writing time for sharing. Notify writers who will present their work that day, and encourage them to think about which piece of text they would like to present.

Explain to children how to listen and respond to the writing they hear. Discuss behaviors that promote good listening, such as eye contact and still bodies.

> Writers must have the opportunity to share their writing with active listeners.

Model for children appropriate responses they might make after hearing a piece of writing. Teach children to make positive remarks and ask constructive questions (e.g., *I was confused at the end. Did your friend go home with you or with her dad?*). Remind them to always thank a writer for sharing his or her work by applauding at the end. A community of writers celebrates each other's work.

Sharing at Home

The community of writers includes the families of your young learners. Each chapter in this book ends with a parent letter and an activity page to send home. Letters begin with a summary of what the community of writers has accomplished recently, and the activity pages offer methods for reinforcing these skills at home. Fill in the blank on each letter with a "complete by" date before reproducing it. Include a copy of the coordinating reproducible activity to help families make writing a part of their routine at home.

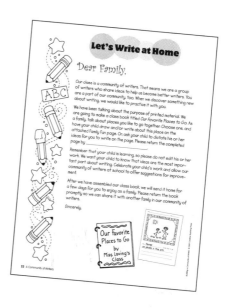

Establish Daily Writing Routines

Ensure that writing time will be productive. When introducing your class to the idea of a community of writers, describe activities that will become routine. Explain what children should do when they need help and you are busy conferencing with another child, and explicitly describe behaviors that are acceptable during writing time. Consider the following suggestions when making your plan.

• Make a variety of writing materials easily accessible to children. Pencils, markers, and crayons are obvious choices for writing tools, but consider additional items that will encourage children to expand their writing. Sticky notes, loose paper, staples, scissors, and tape can all be used to help children add text and illustrations during the revision process.

• If possible, make a small writing kit for each child. Place pencils, an eraser, and markers in a box labeled with the child's name and store it in plain view of the class.

• Prepare several writing booklets for each child. Having small books with several blank pages on hand encourages children to write more. Children will need a new booklet for each story they write. Provide children with paper that features primary writing lines and space for illustrations. To make a booklet, staple the pages between construction paper covers. You may wish to have children place completed writing booklets or works in progress in individual file folders for easy access.

• Establish ground rules for writing time. Remind children that we show respect for other writers when we use quiet voices to discuss our work with others.

Assessment

Portfolios

The best way to assess a writer's growth is to compare pieces of work in a portfolio. Designate a box or other container for each child that can store several writing samples. Sit with each child periodically and point out how he or she has grown as a writer. Give children access to their portfolios so they can learn to evaluate their own writing.

Teacher-Child Conferencing

Individual conferencing helps you contribute to a child's development as a writer while assessing his or her progress. A conference can be as simple as visiting a child who is writing and asking a few questions about the piece. Or it can be a formal arrangement in which you invite a child to meet with you to discuss a particular piece of writing.

To maximize your time together during a conference, keep in mind some important guidelines to help children feel more comfortable while sharing their work.

1. Sit beside the child and use body language that shows he or she has all of your interest and attention. The child should not feel as if he or she is being evaluated.

2. Listen expressively to what the child reads. Writers feel empowered when they recognize their ability to move people with their ideas.

3. Begin with the positive. Comment on all of the things a child is doing to make his or her writing interesting.

4. Identify no more than two aspects of the writing you would like the child to consider. The purpose is not to correct his or her writing, but to explore writing techniques and conventions.

Use the Thoughts About Our Writers' Work reproducible on page 11 to record anecdotal notes about a conference. This allows you to write your observations without distracting the child from the conversation about his or her writing. The Performance Checkoff reproducibles on pages 94 and 95 can help you track student progress.

Community Conferencing

The writing community is enhanced when young writers learn from one another. Facilitate this process by modeling for children how to talk about their own writing and respond to the writing of others. After a mini-lesson, have children work on a piece of writing of their own choosing. Write your own piece as children write. Then, demonstrate how a small group conference might proceed as shown below.

Point to the title of your story. "Grandma to the Rescue by Mrs. Cernek. When I was a girl, we went to my uncle's house for the Fourth of July. He started to spray us with a water hose! I did not like being chased. Grandma noticed I was upset. I watched her go into the house and come out hiding something behind her back. She sneaked up on my uncle and cracked an egg on his head! We all laughed."

"Carly and Sydney will now tell me what they liked about my story." Prompt partners to discuss your writing by giving them a sentence starter such as, "I liked the part when _____."

"Now, Carly and Sydney will tell me what they think I can do to make my story better." Prompt partners to comment on parts of the story they did not understand or suggest something that might be added to make the story more interesting.

"Now it is Sydney's turn to share her story. Carly will be next. Please share your own stories with your small group as Carly, Sydney, and I continue to work together."

Children of various developmental levels might conference with each other, so it is imperative that they are respectful of everyone's writing abilities. Remind children that each member of your writing community is a writer, and writers can use pictures, letters, words, or sentences to tell their stories. Children at all levels can help each other because a story idea is the basis for writing and all children have ideas to share and develop.

Thoughts About Our Writers' Work

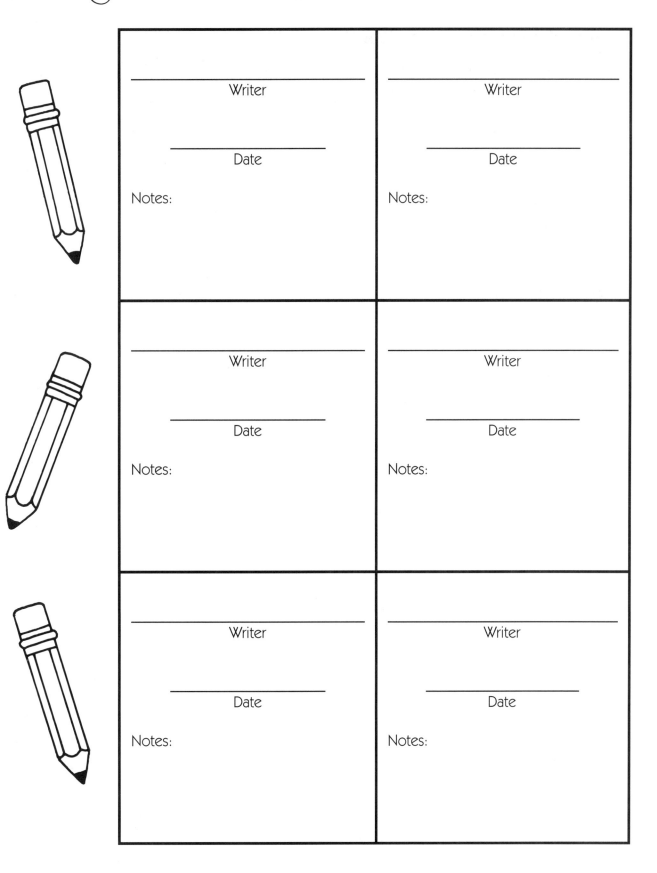

_____
Writer

_____
Date

Notes:

_____
Writer

_____
Date

Notes:

_____
Writer

_____
Date

Notes:

_____
Writer

_____
Date

Notes:

_____
Writer

_____
Date

Notes:

_____
Writer

_____
Date

Notes:

Building a Community of Writers © 2007 Creative Teaching Press

Standards-Based Literacy Practices

Both reading and writing standards are addressed in each unit of study. The Standards Connection at the end of each activity page provides a list of the specific literacy skills covered in the mini-lesson and accompanying activities. Below is an overview of the literacy standards addressed in each Writing Unit.

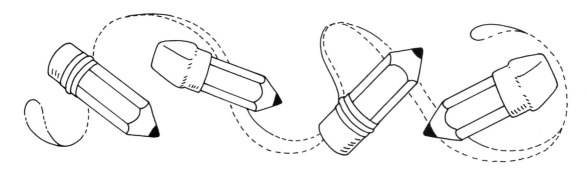

Unit 1: A Community of Writers
• Understand that the purpose of print is to communicate
• Develop vocabulary
• Recognize environmental print
• Recognize the importance of reading in our lives
• Use left-to-write and top-to-bottom direction when reading and writing
Unit 2: The Basics of Our Craft
• Identify main idea
• Use prewriting tools, such as semantic webs and concept maps, to organize ideas and information
• Recognize that a story begins with an idea
• Make connections between personal experiences and story ideas
• Practice generating ideas for writing
• Use illustrations to understand text and to anticipate what will happen next
Unit 3: Getting Started
• Predict what might happen in a story that is read aloud
• Create a story with a beginning, a middle, and an end
• Use descriptive language in writing
• Understand that word choice can shape ideas, feelings, and actions
• Recognize action words as serving a different function from other words
• Identify action words as verbs

Unit 4: Learning About Conventions
• Demonstrate print awareness
• Understand that punctuation is used in all written sentences
• Identify how periods and capital letters are used in writing
• Identify how exclamation points and question marks are used in writing
• Identify how quotation marks are used in writing
• Identify how paragraphs are used in writing

Unit 5: Make Writing Interesting
• Use varied language in writing
• List the sequence of events in a story
• Recognize patterned structures in text
• Recognize time order words
• Recognize the connection between illustrations and text

Unit 6: Parts of a Story
• Recognize that a strong lead creates interest in a story
• Recognize that the main action of a story occurs in the body
• Practice adding details to writing
• Recognize that details make writing more interesting
• Identify details in the body of a story
• Understand the importance of a strong conclusion

Unit 7: Point of View
• Understand that stories can be written from different points of view
• Identify the point of view of a story
• Recognize the characteristics of a journal
• Understand that each author has a writing style
• Distinguish fiction from nonfiction text
• Identify details in nonfiction text

Unit 8: Author & Subject Studies
• Recognize the characteristics of an author's particular style and voice
• Sequence story events
• Evaluate why an author's work is effective
• Share writing samples aloud

A Community of Writers

Help children learn to talk about their ideas and learn how to talk about writing with others. They will feel more comfortable taking risks and expressing themselves.

| MINI-LESSON 1 | Recognizing Print |

READ and THINK

"Welcome, everyone, to our very first writer's workshop. We are a community of writers. That means we are a group of people who have something in common—we like to write!"

"Yes, you are writers. And, our community of writers is going to help you become even better writers! Let's read some of the things writers write."

MATERIALS

• collection of printed materials (e.g., postmarked letter, magazine, book, shopping list)

• basket or decorated box

Invite volunteers to select an example of a printed item from the basket or box, and ask them to describe what they are holding. For example, prompt a child who selects a postmarked letter to say "This is a letter. Someone wrote his or her ideas on a piece of paper, placed the paper in an envelope, and sent it to someone else to read."

"Letters, magazines, books, shopping lists, and other materials with print or writing help us communicate and share our thoughts and ideas with other people."

"In our community of writers, we will do a lot of sharing. When you write, you share your thoughts, feelings, and ideas. When you listen to what someone has written, you share what you like and do not like about the writing, and offer ideas about how to make it better. Our community of writers will help us grow as writers."

WRITE and APPLY

"Find a partner, and search the classroom for printed materials. Then share with our writing community your ideas about what printed material is and what purpose it serves."

Going on a Print Hunt

MATERIALS
- big book
- chart stand or easel

Display a big book on an easel. Teach children the following version of "A-Hunting We Will Go." *A-hunting we will go. A-hunting we will go. We'll take a look inside a book for letters in a row.* Invite a volunteer to open to a page in the book and point to a word. Point to each letter of the word and read it aloud. Then say the word. Emphasize that when you put these letters together in this particular order, they make a word. Repeat the chant and invite other volunteers to point out words in the book.

Wordless Picture Book

MATERIALS
- wordless big book
- chart stand or easel
- sentence strips

Display a wordless big book on an easel. Take children on a "picture walk." As children describe what they see in the illustrations, emphasize that even though there is no print on the page, we can still tell the story. Return to the first page of the book, and invite children to help you write the story. Record the story on sentence strips. As you write children's ideas, emphasize that you are using print to record the story on paper. Display and reread the sentence strips, and congratulate children for their part in using print to tell the story.

A deer found water to drink.

STANDARDS CONNECTION

✐ Recognize print

✐ Understand that the purpose of print is to communicate

✐ Develop vocabulary

Print Is Everywhere

"Welcome, everybody. This is our second writer's work-shop. I am so proud to be a part of such a talented group of writers. It is important to share my ideas about writing with this special community of writers."

"Last time we looked at materials writers write."

Ask children to name materials they examined in the previous lesson.

"Today we will look at printed materials we see every day in our lives." Invite volunteers to select an example of environmental print from the basket or box, and tell them to describe what they are holding and its purpose. For example, prompt a child who selects a paper cup to say something like "This is a paper cup from *McDonald's*. I can see the *M* on the cup. McDonald's starts with *m*." Staple each item to a bulletin board titled We Read Our World!

"Everywhere we go we see printed words. Why do you think restaurants print the name on their cups? *(So people will get to know the name and symbol for the restaurant.)* Tell us about other places you have seen printed words."

MATERIALS
- collection of environmental print (e.g., paper cup with a restaurant logo, candy wrapper, movie ticket stub)
- basket or box
- stapler

"I am going to give each of you a piece of paper. You are going to design a toy. Draw a picture of your toy and, if you would like, write its name below the picture. Be sure the picture and words show or tell people what you would like them to know about the toy you designed. We will then bind our papers together in a class book titled Our Toy Catalog."

Print in Our World

MATERIALS

- magazines
- scissors
- glue sticks
- blue butcher paper

Give pairs of children a magazine, and tell them to cut out samples of print. Have children glue their cutouts to a blue butcher paper circle titled *Print in Our World.*

Display children's work, and explain that these are words we see in our world. Point to the words and read them aloud with children.

Print Scavenger Hunt

MATERIALS

- digital camera
- supplies to assemble a class book

Invite children to join you on a hunt for print. Lead children around the school, and ask them to point out printed material they see. Use a digital camera to photograph the print samples. Print the photographs and assemble them into a book titled *Print in Our School.* Place the book at a reading center, and encourage children to use the book to help them spell words about their school in their writing.

STANDARDS CONNECTION

- ✐ Recognize environmental print
- ✐ Understand that the purpose of print is to communicate
- ✐ Recognize the importance of reading in our lives

What Readers Do

READ and THINK

"We are learning what it means to be a community of writers. We know that our world is filled with printed materials or things that have writing. When you read a sign at your favorite restaurant, you are a reader. When you tell a story about a picture you see, you are a reader. When you put together letters to make words, you are a reader. When you put together words to make sentences, you are a reader. When you put together sentences to read whole pages of a book, you are a reader. Raise your hand if you are a reader. Yes, all of you are readers!"

"In order for our community of writers to grow, we must also become good readers. I am going to read a story titled *Skip to My Lou* written by Nadine Bernard Westcott. Nadine Bernard Westcott is the author of this story."

Before you read aloud, point out the front and back covers of the book. Explain to children that we read a book from the front to the back. We read print left to right, and from the top of the page to the bottom.

Read aloud the story. Emphasize the repeating line *Skip to my Lou, my darling* so children will choral read with you. Point out the text and illustrations in the book as you read.

MATERIALS

• *Skip to My Lou* by Nadine Bernard Westcott (Little, Brown and Company)

I am a reader!

"I am going to place this story in our reading center for you to read during free choice time. Remember, good writers are good readers, and you all are readers! I am going to give each of you a piece of paper. Please draw or write about your favorite part of the story *Skip to My Lou.*"

WRITE and APPLY

"I am going to place this story in our reading center for you to read during free choice time. Remember, good writers are good readers, and you all are readers! I am going to give each of you a piece of paper. Please draw or write about your favorite part of the story Skip to My Lou."

ACTIVITY A

Readers Are as Readers Do

MATERIALS

• bulletin board or chart paper

Teach children the following poem. Have children chant this poem every morning to remind them about the importance of reading. Display the poem on an attractive bulletin board or write it on chart paper for children's reference.

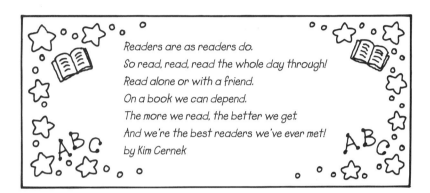

Readers are as readers do.
So read, read, read the whole day through!
Read alone or with a friend.
On a book we can depend.
The more we read, the better we get.
And we're the best readers we've ever met!
by Kim Cernek

ACTIVITY B

Read and Write from Left to Right

MATERIALS

• *Skip to My Lou* by Nadine Bernard Westcott (Little, Brown and Company)

• chart paper

• highlighters (yellow and orange)

Write a few lines from *Skip to My Lou* on a piece of chart paper. Explain to children that when we read we begin at the left side of the page and move to the right side. Use a yellow highlighter to draw an arrow pointing to the right across the first line. Teach children to chant the following verse to the tune of *Skip to My Lou*:

Left, left, left-to-right.
Left, left, left-to-right.
Left, left, left-to-right.
Left-to-right when we read and write!

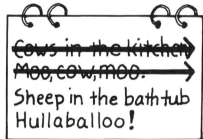

Ask volunteers to draw yellow arrows across the remaining lines of text as you lead the chant again. Tell children that we read and write from left to right across each line until we reach the bottom of the page. Use an orange highlighter to draw an arrow from the top of the page to the bottom.

STANDARDS CONNECTION

🖉 Use left-to-write and top-to-bottom direction when reading and writing
🖉 Recognize the importance of reading in our lives
🖉 Demonstrate print awareness

Use Pictures, Letters, and Words

READ and THINK

"We have talked about all the different things we can read—pictures, letters, words, sentences, and pages of books. Writing is much the same. There are many different ways to write."

"When we write we tell a story on paper. As writers we can use pictures, letters, words, or sentences to write our stories. The most important thing to remember is that we are all writers. Reading and writing take practice, so we must read and write every day."

MATERIALS

- *I Love You* by Jean Marzollo (Scholastic)
- writing booklets (see page 8)

"The story I am going to read for you now is titled *I Love You,* written by Jean Marzollo. She uses words and picture clues to tell her story. Listen carefully and pay close attention to the pictures as I read."

Read aloud the story. Point to the rebus words as you read them aloud. Tell children, "I will place this book at our reading center for you to read at free choice time."

"You are all writers, and you need certain tools to write. Take a look at these special writing books." Display an assortment of writing booklets you have prepared following the directions on page 8. "Use a different book for each new story you would like to write. Take a book now and write a story. Remember, a writer can use pictures, letters, words, or sentences to tell a story on paper."

Writers Are as Writers Do

ACTIVITY A

MATERIALS

• bulletin board or chart paper

Teach children the following poem. Have children chant this poem every morning to remind them about the importance of writing. Display the poem on an attractive bulletin board or write it on chart paper for children's reference.

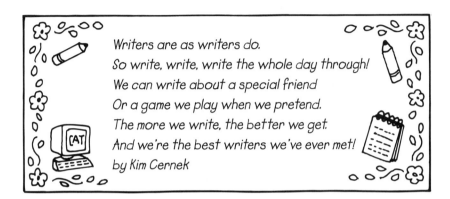

Writers are as writers do.
So write, write, write the whole day through!
We can write about a special friend
Or a game we play when we pretend.
The more we write, the better we get.
And we're the best writers we've ever met!
by Kim Cernek

Writing Like We Read

ACTIVITY B

MATERIALS

• chart paper

Write the frame *Everyone loves a _____.* several times on a piece of chart paper. Invite children to think about their favorite playground equipment, and use these ideas to complete the frame. Draw only a rebus picture for each idea (e.g., swing, seesaw). Write four or five ideas on the chart paper. Then invite children to help you write the words for each idea. Prompt children to sound out the words and write the letters for the sounds they hear. Ask children to help you read aloud the sentences you wrote.

STANDARDS CONNECTION

✐ Use left-to-write and top-to-bottom direction when reading and writing
✐ Recognize that pictures and words communicate ideas
✐ Develop vocabulary

Let's Write at Home

Dear Family,

Our class is a community of writers. That means we are a group of writers who share ideas to help us become better writers. You are a part of our community, too. When we discover something new about writing, we would like to practice it with you.

We have been talking about the purpose of printed material. We are going to make a class book titled *Our Favorite Places to Go.* As a family, talk about places you like to go together. Choose one, and have your child draw and/or write about this place on the attached Family Fun page. Or, ask your child to dictate his or her ideas for you to write on the page. Please return the completed page by _____.

Remember that your child is learning, so please do not edit his or her work. We want your child to know that ideas are the most important part about writing. Celebrate your child's work and allow our community of writers at school to offer suggestions for improvement.

After we have assembled our class book, we will send it home for a few days for you to enjoy as a family. Please return the book promptly so we can share it with another family in our community of writers.

Sincerely,

Building a Community of Writers © 2007 Creative Teaching Press

Name _____ Date _____

The _____ family likes to go

_____

_____

_____.

2 The Basics of Our Craft

All good writing starts with a good idea. Let's focus on where authors get ideas and how they develop them.

MINI-LESSON 1 ## Writing Starts with an Idea

READ and THINK

"Today we are going to talk about what a writer thinks about before he or she puts a story on paper. Writing starts here [point to your mind]. You must have an **idea** for a story before you can write it down on paper."

> **MATERIALS**
> • *Fall Leaves Fall!* by Zoe Hall (Scholastic)

"Take a look at this book by Zoe Hall titled *Fall Leaves Fall!* Look at the cover of the book. What do you think is the writer's idea for the story?"

"When I read this book, I noticed an explanation that tells where Zoe Hall got the idea for this story." Read aloud the last page of the book.

"Before Zoe Hall wrote this story, she spent time thinking about things people like to do in the fall. Then she used words, and an illustrator drew pictures, to tell her story on paper. Think about the main idea—things people do in the fall—as I read this story."

Read aloud the story. Emphasize the details that support the main idea of things people do in the fall.

A story starts with an idea.

WRITE and APPLY

"Before you write today, spend time thinking about some of your story ideas. Choose one idea and think about the details that you will include in your story."

Idea Web

MATERIALS

- *Fall Leaves Fall!* by Zoe Hall (Scholastic Press)
- chart paper

Tell children that writers make a plan before they write. Explain that they choose an idea to write about and then think about the details that support this idea. Ask children to name the main idea of *Fall Leaves Fall!* (i.e., things to do in fall), and write it in the center of a piece of chart paper. Draw a circle around the main idea. Draw three or four lines out from the circle to make a web. Ask children to name some of the details (e.g., *rake leaves, jump in leaves*) that support the main idea. Ask children to retell the story using words from the web. Display the chart paper at the writing center.

Compare leaves — Rake leaves — Things to do in fall — Stomp leaves — Jump in leaves

Idea Jar

MATERIALS

- craft supplies (e.g., stickers, glitter glue, ribbon)
- plastic jar
- strips of colored card stock

Use craft supplies to decorate a plastic jar titled *Idea Jar*. As children share their thoughts, feelings, and anecdotes throughout the day, write them on strips of colored card stock and put them in the idea jar. For example, during a discussion about the book *Fall Leaves Fall!*, a child might mention an apple-picking trip last fall with his or her family. Say *What a great idea for a story! Let's write down this idea and put it in the idea jar.* Invite the child who shared the idea to place the strip in the jar.

Repeat this process throughout the day, and then use the strips in various ways.

- Select a strip from the idea jar, and invite the class to develop the idea.

- Give small groups of children a sheet of butcher paper, and have them write and illustrate the story together.

- Select strips from the idea jar when you need an idea for a piece of writing you are modeling for the class.

STANDARDS CONNECTION

- Identify main idea
- Make predictions based on illustrations
- Use prewriting tools, such as semantic webs and concept maps, to organize ideas and information

Where Writers Get Ideas

"An idea for a story can come from anywhere. You might want to write about your pet or a place you have visited. You could write about something funny that happened to you or a time you felt sad."

MATERIALS
- *Joseph Had a Little Overcoat* by Simms Taback (Viking)
- writing folders (labeled with _____'s *Story Ideas*)

Show children the cover of *Joseph Had a Little Overcoat*. Say "This book titled *Joseph Had a Little Overcoat* was written by Simms Taback. When I read this book, I noticed that on the last page, the author writes a letter to his readers explaining where he got his idea for the story." Read aloud the letter. "Simms Taback used his own words and illustrations to write his version of a favorite song."

"Writers get ideas all the time and often write them down to use later. Of course, not all ideas turn into stories; but the more ideas you have, the more subjects you have from which to choose."

"I am going to give each of you a special folder (labeled *Story Ideas*) with a piece of paper in it. Whenever you think of an idea for a story, write or draw it on the paper. When you fill up your paper, I will give you another one. Use this list whenever you are looking for a new idea for a story."

Idea File

MATERIALS
- magazines
- scissors
- glue
- index cards
- small box

Give pairs of children a magazine. Ask children to cut out any interesting pictures they find. Have children glue each picture on a separate index card. Collect the cards. Show each picture card to the class, and ask children to describe what they see. Write a few of their thoughts on the back of the card. Then place the cards in a small box labeled *Writing Ideas*. Place the box at the writing center, and invite children to select a picture card from the box if they would like a new idea for a story. Remind children that there are words on the back of the card that relate to the picture.

Idea Donations

MATERIALS
- crayons or markers
- envelopes
- decorated box

Have children help you write a letter to other teachers and school helpers asking them to "donate" ideas for your writing workshop. Copy a class set of the letter, and ask children to help you decorate each one.

Have children insert the letters into envelopes and deliver them to teachers, the librarian, the custodian, the principal, and parent volunteers. On the appointed day, lead children to pick up their "donations." When you return to the room, read aloud the ideas and store them in a box labeled *Donate-an-Idea Box*. Use these ideas during shared writing, or encourage children to use these ideas during writing workshop.

Dear School Friend,
  Our community of writers is collecting ideas for our writing workshop. We are looking for memories, dreams, or anything else you think would make a good story. Please donate one idea for pickup on Tuesday at 10:00 a.m.
          Sincerely,
          Mrs. Martin's Class

STANDARDS CONNECTION
- ✐ Recognize that a story begins with an idea
- ✐ Make connections between personal experiences and story ideas
- ✐ Practice generating ideas for writing

Writing Our Ideas

MATERIALS
- *Ribbon Rescue* by Robert Munsch (Scholastic)
- writing folders (see page 26)

"We have spent some time talking about where writers get ideas. Today we are going to think about putting these ideas on paper."

"Take a look at this book titled *Ribbon Rescue* by Robert Munsch. Robert Munsch is a storyteller. He was telling a story to a group of children one day and noticed a girl in the audience who was wearing a dress much like the girl on the book cover. The girl, named Jillian, explained that she is a Mohawk from the Kahnawake reserve, and her dress is a traditional Mohawk costume worn on special occasions. Robert Munsch decided to write a story about Jillian and her special dress."

"We know that the idea for this book came from someone the writer met. After Robert Munsch made a plan for his book, he began to write it down. Let's read the book and see how he turned the idea of a girl wearing a traditional dress into a story."

Read aloud the story. Prompt children to describe how the girl uses the ribbons on her dress to help people who are on their way to a wedding.

"I really like the way Robert Munsch tells a story about something new he saw—the unique dress worn by the Mohawk girl. He thought of some clever ways the ribbons on her dress could be used to help others and wrote about them in this story."

"You now have a special place in your writing folder where you can list ideas you have for stories. Do not forget to add unique or unusual objects that you see. You might be able to tell a story about one of those items. If you are ready to write a new story today, look at the list in your writing folder for an idea for a new story."

My Closet

MATERIALS
- drawing paper
- construction paper
- crayons or markers
- glue sticks

At the top of a sheet of drawing paper write *My closet is the place where I keep...* Copy the paper, and give one to each child. Give each child a large sheet of construction paper. Show children how to fold in both sides to create "closet doors." Help children glue their writing paper inside their "closet." Then invite children to draw a picture of something special they keep in their closet. Read aloud the story starter, and encourage children to complete the sentence. Encourage them to use their best writing.

Our Story Closet

MATERIALS
- chart paper
- envelopes
- crayons or markers
- decorated box

Draw a web on chart paper, and write *Story Closet* in the center. Ask children to name what they keep in their closets. Add their ideas to the chart. Read aloud from the web, and tell children that all of these items could be ideas for stories. Display the web at the writing center. Have each child choose one idea from the list and use it to write a story.

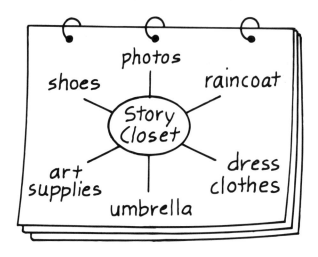

Bind children's stories together in a book titled *Our Story Closet*. Remind children that they can make their own idea webs and keep them in their writing folders.

STANDARDS CONNECTION

✐ Practice generating ideas for writing

✐ Use prewriting tools, such as semantic webs and concept maps, to organize ideas and information

✐ Make connections between personal experiences and story ideas

Illustrations Match Text

READ and THINK

"We have been talking about how a story starts with an idea that a writer writes on paper. The words of a story are called **text**. Another important part of a story is the **illustrations**, or the pictures, that match the text. "

MATERIALS

• *Peter's Chair* by Ezra Jack Keats (Viking)

Illustrations are an important part of a story.

"Take a look at this book by Ezra Jack Keats called *Peter's Chair*. The illustrations in this book match the text, or words, so closely that we can tell most of the story without reading the words. Let's look at the pictures, and you tell me what you see."

Take children on a "picture walk." Prompt them to describe the illustrations as if telling a story (e.g., *Peter is building with blocks, and then the dog knocks down his tower. He is watching his mother take care of a baby and his father paint a purple high chair pink.*). Point out features of the illustrations that add to the story (e.g., *The baby's room and the high chair are pink, so the baby must be a girl. Peter does not seem happy in these illustrations.*).

Read the story. Pause to let children evaluate how well the illustration on each page matches the text. "When we write, we remember to draw illustrations that match the text on the page."

WRITE and APPLY

"When you illustrate your work, think about how well your drawings match your text."

A Picture-Perfect Birthday

- butcher paper
- crayons or markers
- stapler

Write the following six sentences along the bottom of separate sheets of butcher paper:

- *Sarah slipped out of bed and walked downstairs.*
- *The kitchen was dark, but she still found her way.*
- *Sarah turned on the light and saw a gift on the table.*
- *When she turned around, she saw her mom and dad holding a cake.*
- *Her brother and sister appeared and threw confetti in the air.*
- *"Happy Birthday, Sarah!" they all cheered.*

Organize children into six groups. Read aloud the sentence at the bottom of each paper, and ask children to illustrate the sentence in the top half of the paper. Remind children that their illustration should match the text. Staple the six papers together under a blank cover. Read aloud the story and discuss the illustrations on each page. Ask children to add a title to the front cover of the book. Add blank pages to the back of the book, and invite children to help you finish writing the story. Place the book in the writing center, and ask children to draw pictures to match the new text.

Photo Caption Matchup

- camera
- index cards or sentence strips
- pocket chart

Photograph individual and small groups of children while they are active in your classroom. Print the pictures, and write a caption for each picture on a separate index card or sentence strip. Insert the photographs in a pocket chart, and invite children to look at them. Read one caption, and invite a volunteer to insert it in the pocket below the matching photograph. Repeat with the remaining photographs and captions.

We wrote letters to Miss Baker.

STANDARDS CONNECTION

- Use illustrations to understand text and to anticipate what will happen next
- Recognize that illustrations communicate meaning
- Recognize the connection between illustrations and text

Let's Write at Home

Dear Family,

Our community of writers has learned so much in such a short period of time! Now that we know the purpose of print and where to find it, we have started using print to read and write our own stories.

Our current topic focuses on where writers get ideas. The children are beginning to recognize that ideas for stories are everywhere and that a good writer records these ideas for use at a later time.

You can directly support what your child is doing in school by encouraging him or her to think about how the experiences you share as a family could be the basis for stories he or she writes. When you and your child recall a favorite family memory or plan an excursion, simply commenting *That would make a good story!* would help your child see that ideas for stories come from experiences. Your young writer will begin to view the world as a writer does and will be inspired to share his or her experiences and memories in print.

Use the attached sheet _____'s Writing Ideas to begin a new routine of writing down ideas for stories. Post the list on your refrigerator, and help your child record his or her ideas as they arise. Again, you will reinforce this activity every time you remark that you think one of your child's ideas would make a good story.

Have your child return the list to school by _____.
Children will share their ideas with each other and store their list in their writing folder. Our community of writers will encourage each other to consult this list regularly for story ideas. As our year progresses, we will begin to see these ideas take shape in the children's writing.

Sincerely,

Building a Community of Writers © 2007 Creative Teaching Press

_____ 's Writing Ideas

Getting Started

Emphasize ways children can ensure that their writing is complete. Practicing concepts such as beginning, middle, end, and visualization can help with this.

MINI-LESSON 1 | ## Beginning, Middle, and End

READ and THINK

"Every story starts somewhere. This is the **beginning** of the story. Every story must also have an **ending**. Everything that happens in between is the **middle** of the story. Let's look at how Audrey Penn writes a beginning, a middle, and an end for her story titled *The Kissing Hand*."

> **MATERIALS**
> • *The Kissing Hand* by Audrey Penn (Tanglewood Press)

Read aloud the first few pages. "What happens in the beginning of this story?" Discuss with children how Audrey Penn introduces the characters and setting of her story. "What do you think will happen in the middle of the story?"

Oh! I left something out of my story.

Read the middle of the story. Discuss with children the problem that occurs in this part of the text. "How do you think the story will end?"

Read the end of the story. Discuss with children how the problem introduced during the middle of the story is resolved. Then go back and review the beginning, the middle, and the end of the story.

WRITE and APPLY

"When we read, we expect the story to have a beginning, a middle, and an end. Take a look at the story you are writing now. Make sure it has a beginning, a middle, and an end. If something is missing, staple a blank page to add the missing part."

Three-Part Story

MATERIALS
- construction paper
- permanent marker

To show children the parts of a story, fold a piece of construction paper into three equal parts, unfold the paper, and use a permanent marker to trace over the creased lines. Write *beginning, middle,* and *end* at the bottom of separate columns. In the first column, draw a child looking up at a tree where a kite is stuck. In the second column, draw an adult climbing a ladder to retrieve the kite. In the last column, draw the adult and the child flying the kite together. Ask children to use these pictures to tell the beginning, the middle, and the end of this story. Display the story at the writing center, and encourage children to make a similar story chart to plan their own story.

Beginning, Middle, and End Flip Books

MATERIALS
- 12" x 18" (30.5 x 45 cm) construction paper
- 12" x 18" (30.5 x 45 cm) drawing paper
- scissors
- stapler
- 2" (5 cm) black circle cutouts

Fold a piece of construction paper in half lengthwise. Cut the drawing paper in half lengthwise, and place a piece inside the fold. Staple along the crease. Cut the top piece of construction paper to make three equal-sized flaps. Arrange the booklet lengthwise, and attach a circle to the bottom

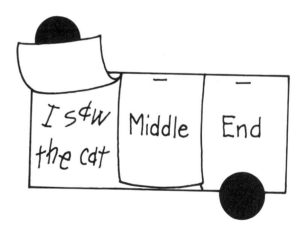

of the first and last flap. Attaching these "wheels" will make the book look like a train car. Write *Beginning, Middle,* and *End* on separate flaps. Make a class set, and give one booklet to each child. Ask children to write the beginning of a story under the first flap, the middle of the story under the second flap, and the end of a story under the third flap. Display children's work on a board titled *Keeping on Track "Write" Through the Beginning, the Middle, and the End!*

Painting a Picture with Words

READ and THINK

"Our community of writers has been talking about how a writer thinks of a story and uses words and pictures to tell it. We know that writing is telling a story on paper. We have talked about where writers get ideas and the importance of matching illustrations with text. Today we will think about how we use words to 'paint a picture' for readers so they can visualize, or see, a picture in their mind."

MATERIALS

• *Grandmother Winter* by Phyllis Root (Houghton Mifflin)

"Look at the cover of this book by Phyllis Root titled *Grandmother Winter*. Tell me what you see." (A grandmother is waving a quilt over the land and dropping snowflakes on the houses, people, and animals below.) "In this story, Phyllis Root imagines that a wise and caring old woman helps pre-pare the world for winter."

"Now I want you to close your eyes and listen while I read. Once in a while I will ask you to open your eyes to look at the illustration to see if it matches the picture you have in your head when you hear the words."

Read aloud from the text and pause on occasion to have children examine illustrations to see if they match the mental picture they get from hearing the text.

"Phyllis Root carefully chooses her words to help you make a picture in your head. I like the part where Phyllis Root writes *When Grand-mother shakes her feather quilt, black bears yawn and burrow into hillside dens*. When I read this, I think about how the bears are preparing to hibernate for the winter. Tell us which words help you make a picture in your head."

WRITE and APPLY

"When you write today, think about the picture your words will paint for your readers."

Scenes from a Snowy Day

MATERIALS

- drawing paper
- crayons or markers
- sentence strips

Give each child a piece of drawing paper. Tell children you will read a sentence to them, and ask them to draw the picture that comes to mind when they hear the words. Say *The red bird perched on the head of the smiling snowman while two spotted rabbits scampered below.* Write the sentence on sentence strips, and display it with children's work on a board titled *Scenes from a Snowy Day.*

Word Pictures

MATERIALS

- various colorful objects (e.g., playing cards, small toys, blocks)
- paper gift bags
- drawing paper
- crayons or markers

Arrange children in pairs, and have them sit back-to-back. Place one object per pair of children in a paper gift bag. Give one child in each pair a piece of paper and some crayons or markers. Ask the other child to take the object out of the bag and describe it to his or her partner. Encourage the child who is speaking to carefully choose words to describe the object. The child with the paper will draw what his or her partner describes. After the activity, invite children to look at the object and the drawing together. Encourage them to determine how well the drawing matches the description.

It is red with wheels.

STANDARDS CONNECTION

- Use descriptive language in writing
- Understand that word choice can shape ideas, feelings, and actions
- Practice visualization

Describing Words

READ and THINK

"A good writer makes a picture with words. Nancy Tafuri carefully chose the words she used in her book titled *What the Sun Sees, What the Moon Sees* to describe what the world is like during the day and at night."

MATERIALS

• *What the Sun Sees, What the Moon Sees* by Nancy Tafuri (Greenwillow Books)

First read *What the Sun Sees*, and then read *What the Moon Sees*. Ask children to describe the barnyard, the owl, the playground, and the children during the day and at the night.

"The writer uses words to describe what the barnyard is like during the day and during the night. We call these **descriptive words** because they describe or tell what something is like. In one part, the author writes *The sun sees crowded barnyards*. In the other part, she writes *The moon sees quiet barnyards*. During the day the barnyard is crowded, but at night it is quiet. Crowded and quiet describe the barnyard at different times of the day."

"Let's go back and look at other words the writer uses to describe the places in her story." Choose text to reread, and emphasize describing words as they appear.

"The way the writer has used describing words in this story helps me make a picture in my mind of what the world is like during the day and at night. She carefully chose the words she would use to 'paint a picture' for her readers."

WRITE and APPLY

"When you write today, think about the words you use to paint a picture for your reader. Try adding describing words to help the reader paint a picture in his or her mind."

ACTIVITY A

Add a Word

MATERIALS

• sentence strips

Fold a sentence strip into thirds. Open the strip, and fold in the right side. Write *a* on the left section and *car* on the flap. Read aloud the words to children, and ask them how to make this description more interesting. Unfold the strip (only *a* will be showing). Ask children to brainstorm words that could describe a car (e.g., *red, shiny, fast*), and write one of the words in the middle section. Rewrite *car* in the third section. Refold the strip, and reread *a car*. Unfold the strip, and read *a shiny car*. Repeat with another sentence strip and set of words.

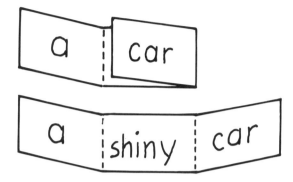

ACTIVITY B

Descriptive Word Files

MATERIALS

• scissors
• magazines
• glue
• file folders
• markers

Make descriptive word files for your writing center. Cut large pictures from magazines, and glue each picture inside separate file folders. Or if you prefer, glue several pictures in each folder according to their themes. Invite children to help you write words that describe each picture. For example, prompt children to list the words *sandy, hot, wet, windy,* and *sunny* for a picture of children playing at the beach. Write the words in neat, large print beside the picture. Close the folder and write *Beach Words* on the cover. Repeat with other pictures. Place the folders at the writing center, and encourage children to use the folders to add descriptive words to their writing.

STANDARDS CONNECTION

✐ Use descriptive language in writing
✐ Understand that word choice can shape ideas, feelings, and actions
✐ Develop vocabulary

Choosing the Right Verbs

READ and THINK

"Denise Fleming won an award called a Caldecott Medal for the illustrations she drew for this book titled *In the Small, Small Pond*." Take children on a "picture walk." "The animals that live in this pond are very active—they like to move! Describe the actions of the animals you see on each page."

MATERIALS

• *In the Small, Small Pond* by Denise Fleming (Henry Holt and Company)

• chart paper

On a piece of chart paper, list the words children suggest to describe the animals' actions. "These wonderful action words you have named are called **verbs**. Verbs are words that describe movement or action. Let's read the verbs or action words Denise Fleming chose to describe the movement of the animals in her story."

Read aloud the text, and emphasize the rhythm and rhyme of the verbs on each page. Point out the way the verbs match the action of the animals in the pictures. "I think the verbs Denise Fleming chose describe very well the movement of the animals in this story. For example, instead of writing *Dragonflies fly*, she wrote *hover, shiver, wings quiver*. These verbs paint a picture in my head of dragonflies using short, quick movements to fly above the pond."

Use words that describe the animals' actions to paint a picture for your audience.

WRITE and APPLY

"When you write today, think carefully about the verbs you use to describe the actions of your characters. Ask yourself, *Do the verbs I have chosen help the reader picture what is happening?*"

ACTIVITY A

You Can Do It, Too!

MATERIALS

- *From Head to Toe* by Eric Carle (HarperCollins)
- index cards
- bag or box

Read aloud *From Head to Toe* by Eric Carle. Ask children to describe the actions of the animals in the book (e.g., bend, raise, wave, clap), and write the words on separate index cards. Place the cards in a bag or box. Arrange children in a circle, and ask a volunteer to select a card. Use the word on the card in the sentence frame: (*Child's name*) can (*verb*) his/her (*body part*). Say the sentence aloud (e.g., **Erin** can **bend** her **neck**). Encourage the child to pantomime the action. Then ask *Can you do it?* Prompt the class to answer *We can do it!* and encourage children to imitate the action. Invite a different volunteer to repeat the frame using a new card until no cards remain.

ACTIVITY B

Animal Actions

MATERIALS

- glue stick
- pictures of animals cut from magazines
- chart paper

Glue pictures of animals in a column along the left margin of a piece of chart paper. Point to the first picture, and ask children to name the animal and imitate the way it moves. Prompt children to use verbs to describe the way the animal moves. Write these words beside the picture and then read them aloud. Repeat with the remaining pictures. Display the chart paper at the writing center, and encourage children to use the verbs associated with each animal in their own writing.

 runs, jumps, sneaks

 slithers, squirms, wiggles

 flies, swoops, dives

 hops, jumps, swims

STANDARDS CONNECTION

- ✐ Recognize action words as serving a different function from other words
- ✐ Identify action words as verbs
- ✐ Develop vocabulary

Let's Write at Home

Dear Family,

Our community of writers grows and grows! As children examine techniques good writers use, they begin to experiment with them in their own writing.

Each of our writing workshops begins with a story. As we read, we focus on an element of writing the writer does well. Recently we have examined how a writer includes a beginning, a middle, and an end in a story.

You can easily reinforce this skill at home when you read together. Simply discuss what happens at the beginning, the middle, and the end of the story. Extend your discussions by imagining a different ending for the story.

Use the attached sheet to help your child organize his or her ideas for a story. Encourage your child to use pictures, letters, or words to record a beginning, a middle, and an end. Invite your child to use the plan to draw and/or write the story on a separate piece of paper. Have your child bring his or her plan and completed story to school by _____.

Remember, our primary concern at this time is to encourage young writers to generate and develop ideas and then record them in print. This process takes time, and conventional handwriting, spelling, and punctuation will come into focus as we progress.

Sincerely,

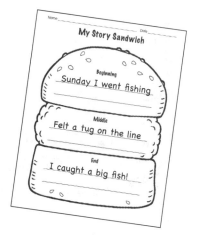

Building a Community of Writers © 2007 Creative Teaching Press

Name _____ Date _____

My Story Sandwich

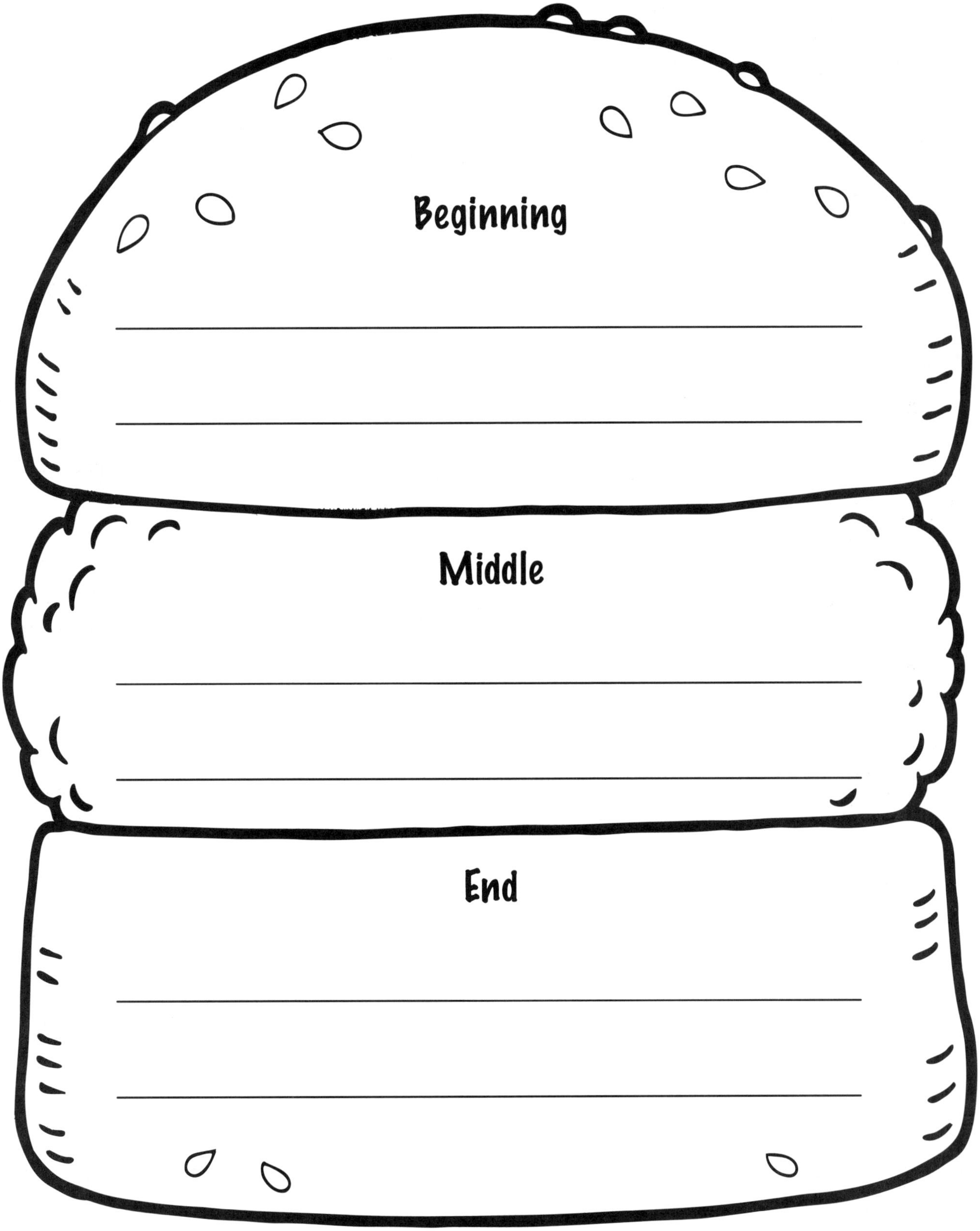

Beginning

_____

_____

Middle

_____

_____

End

_____

_____

Learning About Conventions

4

Celebrate all children's writing, while gently guiding them toward conventional use of punctuation.

MINI-LESSON 1   ## Capitalization and Periods

READ and THINK

"Our writing community has talked a lot about what makes good writing. We know that a story has a beginning, a middle, and an end, and that descriptive words and action verbs paint a picture for the reader. But there are rules we must follow so a reader can understand our words. One rule is that we use signals to tell a reader where one idea ends and where a new idea begins."

MATERIALS

• *If You Give a Mouse a Cookie* by Laura Numeroff (HarperFestival)

Write the first line from *If You Give a Mouse a Cookie* on chart paper.

"Look at the first line from *If You Give a Mouse a Cookie* by Laura Numeroff. *If you give a mouse a cookie, he's going to ask you for a glass of milk.* Notice that the first letter in the first word of the sentence is an **uppercase**, or **capital**, letter. When we write, we always begin a new thought with a capital letter. We let readers know we are finished with that thought by putting a period at the end. That tells the reader to stop and take a breath."

"Now listen as I read the sentence again, and raise your hand when I have finished the whole thought." Reread the sentence, and when children raise their hands at the end of the sentence, say "Very good! You were able to identify when the thought was complete. When we finish writing a thought, we end it with a period. "Then when we read the thought aloud, we pause at this point and take a breath." A period tells the reader that the writer has completed a thought and that a new thought will begin."

"How do you think the next thought will begin? That's right! The next sentence will start with a capital letter." Read the story, and point to the capital letters and periods that begin and end sentences.

WRITE and APPLY

"When you write, use capital letters to begin a new idea and periods to tell readers when you are finished writing an idea. Read your writing aloud to check your work, stopping to take a breath at each period."

Punctuation Detective

MATERIALS

- chart paper
- crayons or markers (orange and yellow)

Write a few sentences on chart paper. You might want to write the directions for your next activity, a message you want to tell your students, or just a funny story. Tell children they are detectives on the lookout for periods and capital letters. Invite volunteers to use an orange crayon or marker to circle the periods on the paper and a yellow crayon or marker to circle the capital letters.

When you are finished putting away your supplies, please line up for an assembly. Remember to keep your hands to yourself, show respect, and thank the speaker for coming to our school.

Make Your Mark

MATERIALS

- markers
- sentence strips
- washable dot markers
- paper towels

Use markers to write simple sentences on separate sentence strips. Omit the periods. Laminate the strips, and place them at a center. Invite children to use dot markers to add a period to the end of each sentence. Use paper towels to clean the strips for other children to use.

STANDARDS CONNECTION

✐ Understand that punctuation is used in all written sentences
✐ Identify how periods and capital letters are used in writing
✐ Demonstrate print awareness

Exclamation Points & Question Marks

READ and THINK

"We have talked about how we can use periods to tell a reader that one thought has ended and another will begin. Today we will talk about the signals a writer uses to show excitement and to indicate that he or she is asking a question."

MATERIALS

• *How Do Dinosaurs Say Goodnight?* by Jane Yolen (The Blue Sky Press)

Writers use symbols to show excitement or to show a question is being asked.

"The characters in Jane Yolen's story *How Do Dinosaurs Say Goodnight?* interact with their parents as they prepare for bed. Listen to this sentence from the story." Read a sentence with an exclamation point and ask "How do you feel when you hear these words? The author wants the reader to read these words with feeling, so she used an **exclamation point** to show this. [Point to the exclamation point in the text.] Whenever you see an exclamation point, it means that you should read with great feeling."

"Whenever you want an answer to something you say, you are asking a question. A writer uses a **question mark** to signal that he or she, or the character in the story, would like an answer. Let's look at the text. I am going to read aloud. Raise your hand when you hear me ask a question." Read a few pages, and point out question marks when they appear.

WRITE and APPLY

"When you write, use an exclamation point when you want the reader to read with feeling. Use a question mark when you want the reader to answer something you or a character asks."

Acting Out

MATERIALS

- *How Do Dinosaurs Say Goodnight?* by Jane Yolen (The Blue Sky Press)
- chart paper

On a piece of chart paper, write sentences from *How Do Dinosaurs Say Goodnight?* Choose questions and exclamations, but omit the punctuation.

Read aloud each sentence. Have children clasp both hands overhead to indicate when a sentence requires an exclamation point at the end, and ask children to shrug their shoulders when a sentence requires a question mark. Add the appropriate ending punctuation after each group of words, and then reread the sentences.

Pretzel Points

MATERIALS

- index cards
- stick pretzels
- cereal O's
- glue

Write interjections and words of praise (e.g., *Wow, Great, Terrific*) on separate index cards. Leave ample space after each word for children to add ending punctuation. Remind children that an exclamation point tells a reader to read with great feeling. Give each child an index card, a stick pretzel, and a cereal O. Have children glue their pretzels and cereal O's after the word in the shape of an exclamation point. When the glue dries, help children read the word on their card with expression.

STANDARDS CONNECTION

- Understand that punctuation is used in all written sentences
- Identify how exclamation points and question marks are used in writing
- Demonstrate print awareness

Quotation Marks

"We have been busy learning about the different signals or **punctuation marks** writers use to show a reader how to read text. Martin Waddell uses periods, exclamation points, and question marks in his story titled *Owl Babies*."

> **MATERIALS**
> • *Owl Babies* by Martin Waddell (Candlewick Press)

"In this story, three baby owls named Sarah, Percy, and Bill talk with each other while their mother is away from their nest searching for food. Martin Waddell uses special marks to indicate which words the owl babies are saying aloud. These are **quotation marks**, and writers use them when characters have a conversation with each other. Raise your hand when you hear me read something that one of the owl babies is saying aloud."

Read aloud the book. Emphasize the dialogue between the owl babies. When children raise their hands, point out the quotation marks in the text. "Notice that there are two sets of quotation marks—one at the beginning and one at the end. They enclose each sentence or question the owls speak aloud."

"When you read *Owl Babies* during free choice time, look for periods, exclamation points, question marks, and quotation marks the writer uses to help the reader read the text."

"You might like to review some of the stories you have written. Do any of the characters say something aloud? If so, add quotation marks to signal this to the reader."

That's What I Said!

MATERIALS

- chart paper
- yellow crayons or markers

Ask one child a question and record his or her exact words on chart paper. Explain to children that in a story, the exact words a character speaks are enclosed in quotation marks. Add quotation marks around the words spoken by the child. Ask several more children a question and repeat the same procedure. Then invite volunteers to use a yellow crayon or marker to circle the quotation marks on the chart paper.

Bubble Talk

MATERIALS

- *Don't Let the Pigeon Drive the Bus!* by Mo Willems (Hyperion Books for Children)
- chart paper

Read aloud *Don't Let the Pigeon Drive the Bus!* Explain to children that whatever the pigeon says aloud is in a speech bubble. Write the words from one speech bubble on chart paper. Ask a volunteer to use quotation marks to enclose the words. Ask them to identify who is speaking these words in the story. Add a comma in the appropriate place and include the words *said the pigeon*. Repeat with another line of text that appears in a speech bubble in the story.

STANDARDS CONNECTION

✎ Understand that punctuation is used in all written sentences
✎ Identify how quotation marks are used in writing
✎ Demonstrate print awareness

Paragraphs

READ and THINK

"In addition to using proper punctuation, there are other things we can do to help a reader understand what we have written. We put spaces between words and sentences to separate them. Sometimes we will write several sentences that tell about or have to do with the same idea. This group of sentences is called a **paragraph**. All the sentences go together to tell about the same thing."

MATERIALS

• *Blueberries for Sal* by Robert McCloskey (Viking)

"When writers begin a paragraph, they **indent** the first word. This means that they leave extra space between the left side of the page and where they begin the first word. When you see an empty space in front of the first word in a paragraph, you know the writer is going to write about something new."

"Listen as I read Robert McCloskey's story titled *Blueberries for Sal*." Read aloud the first page of *Blueberries for Sal*, and point out for children how the text is divided into two paragraphs. "The first paragraph reveals the characters (Mother and Little Sal) and where the story takes place (Blueberry Hill). The next paragraph tells about what they are doing (picking blueberries to can for the winter time)." Continue to read aloud from the story, showing children the text so they can make the connection that new paragraphs signal a change in topic.

"Indent each paragraph to signal that you are writing about something new."

WRITE and APPLY

"If you would like to make a story you are writing easier to read, separate your sentences into paragraphs, and be sure to indent—leave a space—at the beginning of each. To help you decide where to start the first word, place two fingers along the edge of your page before you start to write."

Berry Different Paragraphs

ACTIVITY A

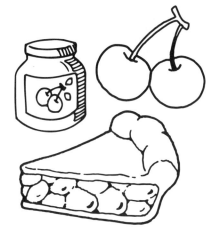

MATERIALS

• chart paper

At the top of a piece of chart paper, write *"Berry" Different Paragraphs.* Tell children they are going to practice recognizing when to start a new paragraph by helping you write about different kinds of berries. On the first line of the chart paper, write "I picked some cherries."

Point out how you indented this sentence, and ask children to help you think of details about the cherries to finish the paragraph (e.g., *I baked a tart and tasty pie; I made a tangy jam.*). After children have composed three sentences, tell them you would like to write about picking strawberries. Ask them what you should do to introduce a new topic. Continue writing paragraphs about picking different berries (raspberries, blackberries, etc.) until children can direct you to start a new paragraph each time you change topics.

Noticing New Paragraphs

ACTIVITY B

MATERIALS

• *The Snowy Day* by Ezra Jack Keats (Puffin)

• *Magic Spring* by Nami Rhee (Putnam)

• *When Lightning Comes in a Jar* by Patricia Polacco (Philomel Books)

• *Toot & Puddle: The New Friend* by Holly Hobbie (Little, Brown and Company)

Place books that demonstrate proper paragraphing at a reading center. Ask children to notice each time a new paragraph begins and think about how the topic changes with the new paragraph. Encourage children to use this convention in their own writing.

STANDARDS CONNECTION

✐ Identify how paragraphs are used in writing

✐ Understand that the purpose of print is to communicate

✐ Demonstrate print awareness

Let's Write at Home

Dear Family,

Our community of writers has made great progress very quickly. We spend a lot of time examining good writing and have demonstrated what we have learned in our own writing. As we become better writers, we become better readers, too.

We have begun talking about how writers use conventions, or specific rules, for writing. At this time, we are concentrating on punctuation. We have learned the role of the period, exclamation point, question mark, and quotation mark.

The best way you can help is to point out the function of punctuation as you read aloud at home. As you read, remark that a period helped you know when an idea was complete. Ask your child why he or she thinks the author chose to use an exclamation point after a particular sentence. Discuss what to expect at the first sign of quotation marks.

It is not necessary to point out every mark you see as you read. Rather, point out marks on occasion, and encourage your child to express observations about the conventional punctuation he or she sees.

The attached page, Punctuation Exploration, will give you a good place to begin your punctuation practice. Please have your child return it to school by _____.

Sincerely,

Name _____ Date _____

Punctuation Exploration

Read these sentences, and discuss the punctuation that follows each one.

I am not sure what to wear today.

Is it going to rain today?

Look at that giant cloud!

Now, add punctuation you think works best to the end of each sentence.

Where is my rain hat

I think I left it at school

Oh, no

Read the words below, and talk about the punctuation marks you see.

"If it rains today, what will happen to our picnic?" asked Chris.

"We'll have the picnic another day, I guess," replied Alex.

"But I looked forward to this all week!" exclaimed Chris.

"Don't give up hope," responded Alex. "I think I have an idea."

Make Writing Interesting

5

Model for children how to add interest to their writing with patterns of events, repeating lines, and more. Children will love exploring how to do this in their own writing.

MINI-LESSON 1 **Making Sentences More Interesting**

READ and THINK

"Listen to a story I wrote."

"I like me. I like to draw. I like to ride. I like to read. I like to eat."

MATERIALS
• *I Like Me!* by Nancy Carlson (Viking)

"When I reread my story, I notice that I use the words *I like* over and over again. I think a reader might be more interested in my story if I added some other words to the sentences."

"When I read *I Like Me!* by Nancy Carlson, I thought of some ways to make my sentences more interesting. As you listen to the text, think about what makes this writer's sentences interesting."

Are my sentences interesting?

Read aloud the first few sentences. Note that even though the author begins most of her sentences with *I*, she adds other words to make the sentences more interesting. "Instead of writing *I like to draw*, Nancy Carlson wrote *I draw beautiful pictures.* And, instead of writing *I like to ride*, Nancy Carlson wrote *I ride fast.*"

"I like these sentences because they tell more about what she can do and how."

WRITE and APPLY

"When you write today, think about how your sentences will sound to your reader. Think about whether you have used the same words over and over again. Think about ways to make your sentences more interesting."

Look at These Lists!

MATERIALS
- chart paper

Invite children to help you make a list of words they can use in their writing. Choose a topic, such as *ways to move*, and write it at the top of a piece of chart paper. Ask children to name ways of moving (e.g., running, hopping, rolling, creeping), and write them on the paper. Other categories could include *words for "big" sounds you hear* and *texture words*. Use this opportunity to introduce to children new vocabulary words and the concept of synonyms. Display the chart paper lists at the writing center. Reread lists from time to time to encourage children to use these words in their writing.

Sentence Additions

MATERIALS
- colored sentence strips
- scissors
- tape

Emphasize to children that good writers always go back and check their work to see if something should be added or taken away. Write on a sentence strip *The girl went home.* Ask children to name a word that could describe the girl (e.g., *happy*), and write it on a different colored sentence strip. Cut apart the sentence strips and tape the word in the gap to make a new sentence (i.e., *The happy girl went home.*). Prompt children to think of a different verb (e.g., *skipped*), write it on a sentence strip of another color, and add it to the sentence. Read aloud the new sentence. Discuss with children the difference between the original sentence and the revised sentence.

STANDARDS CONNECTION

- ✐ Use varied language in writing
- ✐ Understand that word choice can shape ideas, feelings, and actions
- ✐ Develop vocabulary

Transitional Words

READ and THINK

"Let me tell you a short story. Then tell me what you think about it."

"Charlie needed a new coat. Charlie bought some fabric. Charlie cut the fabric. Charlie sewed the fabric. Charlie wore his coat. Charlie was happy."

MATERIALS

• *Charlie Needs a Cloak* by Tomie dePaola (Aladdin)

• chart paper

Prompt children to say that each line begins with the same word. "I think my story would be much more interesting if I used different words to begin each sentence. Let's look at how Tomie dePaola does this in a story he wrote titled *Charlie Needs a Cloak*."

Read the story, and emphasize the transitional words that begin many of the sentences. "In this story, the writer explains how to do something. He tells how to make a cloak, or coat without sleeves. Let's go back and look for words he uses to help connect one sentence to the next." Reread the text, and write transitional words (i.e., *so, then, after*) on chart paper. "The writer uses these words to help the reader know that these are steps that follow each other."

A writer uses words like "so," "then," and "after" to explain events.

"I noticed that sometimes Tomie dePaola uses either the word *Charlie* or *he* in a sentence. Remember when I told you a story and every sentence began with *Charlie*? That started to bother me a bit when I heard that name over and over again. We know that we can use both *Charlie* and *he* to make the story easier to follow. "

WRITE and APPLY

"Think about something you know how to do well. Write this idea in your writing folder. When you are ready to write a new story, think about writing one that explains how to do this special activity. Remember to use words that make your sentences clear and interesting."

First, Next, Then, and Last

ACTIVITY A

Write the following on chart paper: *Draw a circle. Add two eyes. Add a nose. Add a mouth.* Read aloud the sentences, and ask children to help you add words to connect one sentence to the next. Prompt children to add *first, next, then,* and *last* to each successive line. Write each word on a separate sticky note, and ask children to attach the notes to the correct places on the chart paper. Give each child a piece of paper. Tell children to follow the directions as you reread them. Then ask them to write about the character they have just drawn. Encourage children to use sticky notes to add words and ideas to their stories to make them more interesting.

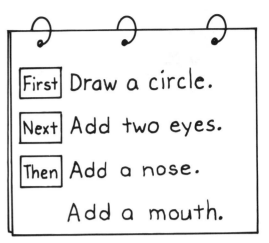

Life Cycle Poster

ACTIVITY B

Divide a poster board into four sections. Draw a seed under the ground in the first box. Draw a sprout emerging from the ground in the next box. Draw a stem with leaves in the ground in the third box. Draw a flower in the ground in the last box. Ask children to describe the life cycle of the flower they see in the pictures. Write their words on a piece of chart paper. Emphasize time order words the children use. Write *first, next, then,* and *last* in separate boxes on the poster board, and display it near the writing center. Remind children to use these time order words in their writing.

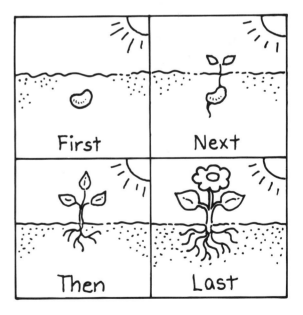

STANDARDS CONNECTION

- ✐ List the sequence of events in a story
- ✐ Use varied language in writing
- ✐ Recognize time order words (e.g., first, next, last)

Patterns

READ and THINK

"We have been talking about where writers get ideas and how to make our writing easy to read. Today let's think about different ways to put together the pieces of a story to make it interesting."

"One way to interest readers in a story is to use a pattern. We know that a pattern repeats itself. Take a look at our calendar and describe a pattern you see." Discuss patterns of colors and shapes on the calendar. "A pattern in a story is very similar, only this time words or an idea are repeated."

Patterns in writing help get a reader's attention

"Take a look at this book by Esphyr Slobodkina titled *Caps for Sale*. Read the first page. The writer has already used a pattern. She repeats the words 'then a bunch of...' three times to describe each color hat the peddler wears. The writer could have simply written *First he had on his own checked cap, then a bunch of gray, brown, and blue caps,* but it was much more interesting to hear the words '*then a bunch of...*' repeated three times."

"I think this pattern is interesting because it helps me paint a picture in my mind. I get a better idea of how tall the stack of caps on the peddler's head is when Esphyr Slobodkina lists each color one by one."

"Let's read on and look for other patterns." As you read, pause to discuss the repeating line *Caps! Caps for sale! Fifty cents a cap!* and the recurring description of the hats' colors. As you read on, you may also wish to discuss how the pattern of words and actions between the peddler and the monkeys helps you imagine mischievous monkeys and a very clever peddler.

WRITE and APPLY

"You might want to think about using a pattern when you write. Remember that a pattern can be words or actions that are repeated."

Patterned Prose

MATERIALS
• chart paper

Draw a two-column chart on chart paper. Ask children to name fairy tales they know (e.g., "Goldilocks and the Three Bears," "The Three Little Pigs"), and list them in the left column. Read the title of the first fairy tale. Ask children to describe the pattern that appears in the story, and write it in the right column. Repeat with the remaining fairy tales. Display the chart at the writing center, and encourage children to write their own patterned story.

Tales	Pattern
Goldilocks and the Three Bears	Mama Bear Papa Bear Baby Bear
The Three Little Pigs	I'll huff, and I'll puff, and I'll blow your house down!

Patterns with Parents

MATERIALS
• *Alligator Baby* by Robert Munsch (Scholastic)
• writing booklets (see page 8)

Read aloud *Alligator Baby*. In the story, parents who are expecting a child keep bringing home the wrong baby. Ask children to identify the pattern in the story (i.e., every time the parents go to the zoo, they bring home an animal baby instead of a human baby). Remind children that patterns help us predict what will happen next. Give children a writing booklet (see page 8), and ask them to write a patterned story about a child whose parents go out to buy him or her gym shoes and keep coming back with shoes other than sneakers (e.g., diving fins, snow boots, ice skates). Invite children to read aloud their patterned stories.

STANDARDS CONNECTION

✏ Recognize patterned structures in text
✏ List the sequence of events in the story
✏ Predict what might happen in a story that is read aloud

Repeating Lines

READ and THINK

"Many of the books we read have patterns. We know that a pattern is something that repeats itself. Sometimes the pattern in a story is a group of words repeated over and over again. This is called a repeating line. The repeating line for our next story appears right on the cover."

MATERIALS

• *Bear Wants More* by Karma Wilson (Margaret K. McElderry Books)

Display the book. "This book by Karma Wilson is titled *Bear Wants More*. Let's read the story and think about why the writer chose to repeat the line *Bear wants more* several times in the story."

Read the book all the way through. Reread the book, and pause to discuss which text feature changes throughout the story. "I noticed that the first time the repeating line appears in the story, the print is very small. The print for the repeating line gets bigger every time it appears. I think the writer does this so the reader will understand just how much a bear can eat!"

"Sometimes the repeating line changes a bit, too, but it always includes the words '*wants more.*' I think the repeating line works well in the book because it helps me focus on each animal that helps feed the bear. Whenever we see the repeating line, a new animal appears on the next page. Let's take a look." Flip through the book. Point to each repeating line and the illustration of a new animal on the next page.

"So we see that repeating lines help us organize a story and make it more interesting to read."

WRITE and APPLY

"Look back at some of the stories you have written, and check to see if you have used a repeating line. If not, think about whether you could add a repeating line to one of your stories or include one in the next story you write."

A Repeating Line Revue

MATERIALS

• none

Discuss with children songs they know that have repeating lines (e.g., "Skip to My Lou," "Five Little Monkeys Jumping on the Bed," "There Were Ten in the Bed"). Choose one of the songs to sing, and invite children to help you make up a dance or movement to perform whenever the line is repeated. Sing the song, and exaggerate the movement that coordinates with the repeating line.

> No more monkeys jumping on the bed!

Looking in Literature for Repeating Lines

MATERIALS

• *The Mouse Who Cried Cat* by Rozanne Lanczak Williams (Creative Teaching Press)

• *Five Little Monkeys Jumping on the Bed* by Eileen Christelow (Clarion Books)

• *From Head to Toe* by Eric Carle (HarperCollins)

• *The Grouchy Ladybug* by Eric Carle (HarperCollins)

• *I Know a Shy Fellow Who Swallowed a Cello* by Barbara S. Garriel (Boyds Mills Press)

Place books that feature repeating lines at a reading center. Invite children to identify the repeating lines in the text. Encourage them to use repeating lines in their own writing.

> These lines repeat. "The cat is coming! The cat is coming! Run away and hide!"

STANDARDS CONNECTION

✐ Recognize patterned structures in text

✐ Recognize the connection between illustrations and text

✐ Understand that word choice can shape ideas, feelings, and actions

Let's Write at Home

Dear Family,

Many of the picture books you read with your child have repeating patterns. A character might repeat an action, or lines of text might repeat over and over again. These patterns add interest to the story and also help your child become a better reader. Children can predict when words will repeat in a story. They will anticipate these words and begin to study how the words appear in print.

Use the attached sheet, Find a Pattern, to help your child respond to a pattern book you have read this week. Have your child return the sheet to school by _____. In order to help you locate books that are appropriate for the assignment, I have listed authors who frequently use patterns and repeating lines in their work. Take some time this week to explore this technique with your child.

Eric Carle (*The Very Hungry Caterpillar*)

Jonathan London (*Froggy Plays in the Band*)

Robert Munsch (*Alligator Baby*)

Karma Wilson (*Bear Wants More*)

We will continue to learn about how stories are organized with a beginning, a middle, and an end and feature patterns and repeating lines to make them more interesting. As we read like writers and write like readers, our skills in both areas grow and grow!

Sincerely,

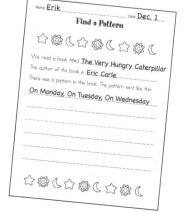

Name _____ Date _____

Find a Pattern

We read a book titled _____.

The author of the book is _____.

There was a pattern in this book. The pattern went like this:

_____

_____

_____

_____

_____

_____

Parts of a Story

6

Go beyond teaching children beginning-middle-end. Model specific ways children can bring their writing to life.

Great Leads

READ and THINK

"Imagine you are at the grocery store with your parents and they allow you to pick out a box of cereal. How will you decide which box to choose?" Discuss with children how the packaging on the box makes you want to see what is inside.

MATERIALS

• *Wemberly Worried* by Kevin Henkes (Greenwillow Books)

How will I get a reader's attention?

"A colorful, interesting picture and a pleasing name make you want to find out what's inside the cereal box. The opening, or **lead**, of a good story is a lot like a cereal box. If the beginning of the story is exciting, it will grab the reader's attention."

"Let's read the story *Wemberly Worried* by Kevin Henkes. Take a look at the cover. Who do you think this is? How does Wemberly look?" (Wemberly looks worried.) "Let's look at the first page. The first sentence or sentences of a story are called the lead." Read the first line: Wemberly worried about everything.

"This lead makes me want to know what Wemberly is worried about. What are some things you think Wemberly worries about?" Invite a few volunteers to share their answers.

"Let's read the story and examine how Kevin Henkes keeps us interested in his lead (*Wemberly worried about everything*)." Read the first 20 pages of the book. As you read, emphasize all the ways Wemberly worries.

WRITE and APPLY

"If you are ready to begin a new story during writing time, you might want to think about the lead for your story. Choose words that will make readers interested in what happens next."

64 Parts of a Story

Looking at Leads

MATERIALS

• chart paper

Write the following pairs of sentences on chart paper:

Sam wore my coat home from school./Why did Sam have to buy the same coat I have?

Aww! Not again./My sister spilled her milk on my pants.

Life will never be the same in our house./We have a new baby.

Read aloud each pair of sentences. Ask children to choose the one in each pair they think sounds more interesting. Put a star beside their choice for the best sentence of each pair. Discuss elements of a good lead (e.g., asks a question, states a problem, makes a statement that causes the reader to want to know more). Display the chart paper at the writing center, and encourage children to use one of the three good leads to write a story during writing time.

Box of Leads

ACTIVITY B

MATERIALS

• shoe box
• index cards

Invite children to help you think of interesting leads to store in a box labeled *Our Box of Leads*. Encourage them to think of questions (e.g., *Where did Spot go now?* or *How did you get here?*), problems (e.g., *It was time for my soccer game, and I could not find my shoe.*) and sounds (e.g., *Ding-dong!* or

Clip clop. Clip clop.). Write children's ideas on index cards, and place them in the box. Tell them to select a card from the box when they need a story starter or an idea for shared writing. Remind children that these are good leads because these are the true elements of a good lead.

STANDARDS CONNECTION

✎ Recognize that a strong lead creates interest in a story
✎ Understand that word choice can shape ideas, feelings, and actions
✎ Recognize that details make writing more interesting

Body of Action

"We know that a good story has a beginning, a middle, and an end. We also know that a great lead comes at the beginning of a story. Another word that describes the middle of a story is **body**. The body of a story is the main part. It is where the main action of a story happens."

"This story by Sheridan Cain, titled *The Crunching Munching Caterpillar*, is a good example of what the body of a story should look like."

Read the first two pages of the story, and discuss the lead. Point out that the body of the story follows. As you read, comment on the animals with wings that the caterpillar meets. Read through the part where the caterpillar is dreaming.

"We have just read the body of the story. During this part of the story, the caterpillar meets three different creatures with wings. We learn that the caterpillar wishes he had wings, too." Read the conclusion.

"Notice that the beginning and the ending of the story are much shorter than the body of the story where most of the action happens."

> **MATERIALS**
> • *The Crunching Munching Caterpillar* by Sheridan Cain (Tiger Tales)

> The body of a story is where the action happens.

"As you write, think about the body of your story. Remember that most of the action of a story happens in the body."

Body Builders

MATERIALS

- undeveloped story (similar to one shown)
- writing paper
- tape

Read aloud to children an undeveloped story, and ask them to help you add more details to the body to make it more interesting. Show children how to use additional sheets of paper and tape to add ideas to the story. Emphasize that a good writer always rereads a story and adds text when necessary to make a story more interesting.

EveryBODY Write!

MATERIALS

- writing paper

Write a beginning to a story (e.g., *The carnival was in town, so I went with my family.*) at the top of the page. Write an ending for the story (e.g., *I can't wait until the carnival returns next year!*) along the bottom of the page. Make a copy of this paper for each child. Give each child a paper, and read aloud the beginning and the end. Prompt children to say that the middle or body of the story is missing. Ask children to write the body of the story, and encourage them to share their stories with each other.

> The carnival was in town, so I went with my family.
> We ate ctn cndy and rod dizy ridz. Then I wn 4 2tuff anml.
> I can't wait until the carnival returns next year.

STANDARDS CONNECTION

- Recognize that the main action of a story occurs in the body
- Identify details in the body of a story
- Practice adding details to writing

Adding Details

READ and THINK

"Every story has a beginning, a middle, and an end. The beginning of a story has a lead, and the middle of a story is called the body. A good writer spends time choosing words for the lead and body of a story that are interesting to readers."

MATERIALS

• *The Seven Silly Eaters* by Mary Ann Hoberman (Harcourt Brace)

What details could I add to make my story more interesting?

"Adding details or information to the body of a story also adds interest. When I read this story titled *The Seven Silly Eaters* by Mary Ann Hoberman, I was very interested in the illustrations and text because they are filled with details, or information, that helped me 'paint a picture' in my head."

Read aloud the story, and pause to comment on the text and illustrations. "Every time we meet a new Peters child, we learn that he or she will only eat one kind of food, and it is always different from what the other children eat. I can see in the illustrations and hear in the text that Mrs. Peters works very hard to give each of her children what they want. I also notice that by the end of the book, Mrs. Peters is very tired from making seven different meals for each of her seven children all day long!"

"The details of the story come together at the end when we see that all of the children's favorite foods mixed together made one special birthday cake for their mother."

WRITE and APPLY

"When you write today, think about the details, or information, you can add to make your story more interesting. Make sure you include all of the details a reader will need to understand and enjoy your story."

It's All in the Details

MATERIALS
- chart paper

Draw an idea web on a piece of chart paper. Write *Packing for the Beach* in the center circle. Tell children that *Packing for the Beach* is the main idea for a story. Ask children to help you add details about packing for the beach, and write them on the web. Review the list, and explain to children that sometimes it helps to use a web to organize our ideas before we write. Remind children that adding details to a main idea makes writing more interesting.

Sorting Through the Details

MATERIALS
- wooden puzzles
- paint
- paintbrush
- writing paper
- tape

Paint the back of a puzzle one solid color. Repeat with a new puzzle and a different color paint. Organize children into small groups. Mix the pieces from all the puzzles together. Assign each group a color, and have children search for the puzzle pieces that match. Tell each group to assemble their puzzle and write a story about the picture they see. Explain to children that the pieces of the puzzle are like the details of a story. You put the pieces or details together to make the big picture or whole story. Display children's stories with their puzzles, and place them at a center. Encourage children to look at the puzzles and read the corresponding stories.

The chimp
The chimp's name is Alfe. We like to watch him do tricks, like jugle and imtat peple. He mad us laugh. by Carly and Simon

STANDARDS CONNECTION

- 🖉 Identify details in the body of a story
- 🖉 Recognize that details make writing more interesting
- 🖉 Practice adding details to writing

Big Finish

READ and THINK

"We have thought about how to get a reader interested in our story by writing a good lead. We have also discussed ways to keep our reader interested by organizing the body of our story and then adding details. The way a story ends, or its **conclusion**, is just as important as how it begins."

MATERIALS
• *Shy Charles* by Rosemary Wells (Viking)

"Take a look at this book titled *Shy Charles* by Rosemary Wells. We can see from the cover that Charles is shy because he won't even look at the woman who is offering him cake. Let's learn a little more about this shy Charles."

Read the first page. "In the very first line of the book the author tells us that even though Charles is shy, he is happy." Continue reading and point out the character's shy behaviors.

> The end of a story is just as important as the beginning.

"I am noticing that Charles doesn't mind being shy, but his parents are a bit frustrated with him." As you read, emphasize instances of Charles's shyness that annoy his parents.

Read along, but stop at the page where Charles notices that the babysitter has fallen down the stairs. "I wonder what Charles will do now that his babysitter is hurt." Read the two pages. "Charles certainly is not acting shy now. He comforts Mrs. Block with kind words and calls the ambulance. This emergency must have cured Charles of his shyness."

Read the remaining pages. "This book ends with one small but very important word—*Zero!* It seems to me that Charles has proven that he can interact with people when necessary, but he chooses to be shy. I like this ending because it surprised me. I also like that it ends with one simple word that says a whole lot."

WRITE and APPLY

"Review some of the stories you have written, and think about whether or not you have a clear, strong ending for your story."

How Will It End?

MATERIALS

• different versions of "Goldilocks and the Three Bears"

Read several adaptations of "Goldilocks and the Three Bears" with your class. Compare and contrast different versions of the story. Ask children to explain why they like or do not like the conclusions of the stories. Invite children to help you think of different endings to the story. Suggest to children that they could write this story with a different conclusion during their writing time.

Goldilocks could have become friends with the bears.

Pourquoi Tales

MATERIALS

• *How Chipmunk Got His Stripes* by Joseph Bruchac (Dial Books)

• *A Story, a Story* by Gail E. Haley (Aladdin)

• *Why Mosquitoes Buzz in People's Ears: A West African Tale* by Verna Aardema (Dial Books)

Explain to children that **pourquoi** tales explain why things are the way they are and usually describe something in nature. For instance, a pourquoi tale might explain how a chipmunk got his stripes. *Pourquoi* [pronounced por-kwa] means "why" in French. Choose a story from the list, read it aloud, and ask children to identify the explanation that appears in the ending of the book. Encourage children to create their own pourquoi tales about things that are familiar to them. Or, write one together as a class.

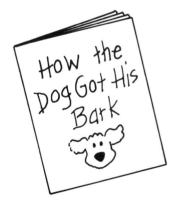

How the Dog Got His Bark

Why a Bunny Hops

STANDARDS CONNECTION

✐ Understand the importance of a strong conclusion

✐ Understand that word choice can shape ideas, feelings, and actions

✐ Create a story with a beginning, a middle, and an end

Let's Write at Home

Dear Family,

Our community of writers has been busy thinking about the ways stories are organized. We have looked at the ways writers make the beginning, the middle, and the end of their stories more interesting.

We know that a good story begins with a great lead. A writer uses a lead to get the reader interested in reading the rest of the story.

We also learned about how to make the middle, or body, of a story more interesting. We discussed how to add details to explain what happens in a story.

Finally, we discussed the importance of the ending, or conclusion, of a story. We know that the ending must be as interesting as the lead.

When you read at home, talk about the way a writer chooses to begin and end a story, and discuss the details that help you understand what is happening in the middle of a story.

The attached sheet, Parts of a Story, gives you an opportunity to write a story together. Have fun thinking about the lead, the body, and the conclusion for your story. Have your child return the paper to school by _____.

Sincerely,

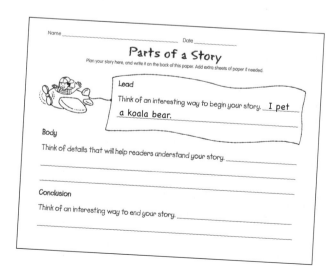

Name _____ Date _____

Parts of a Story
Plan your story here, and write it on the back of this paper. Add extra sheets of paper if needed.

Lead
Think of an interesting way to begin your story. I pet a koala bear.

Body
Think of details that will help readers understand your story. _____
_____
_____

Conclusion
Think of an interesting way to end your story. _____
_____

Building a Community of Writers © 2007 Creative Teaching Press

Name _____ Date _____

Parts of a Story

Plan your story here, and write it on the back of this paper. Add extra sheets of paper if needed.

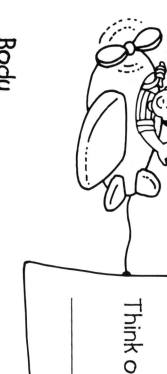

Lead

Think of an interesting way to begin your story. _____

Body

Think of details that will help readers understand your story. _____

Conclusion

Think of an interesting way to end your story. _____

Point of View

7

Children's enthusiasm for writing will grow as they learn to think about a story's point of view. Use these activities to foster creative writing and comprehension.

MINI-LESSON 1

"Watching" a Story

READ and THINK

"The **narrator** of a story can be a character in the story, or it can be someone who 'watches' the story happen and then tells about it. *Harry the Dirty Dog*, written by Gene Zion, is a funny story told by someone who is 'watching,' or observing, what is going on and tells the reader about it."

> **MATERIALS**
> • *Harry the Dirty Dog* by Gene Zion (HarperCollins)

Read the story aloud. As you read, discuss with children how the narrator describes the characters, setting, and plot of the story.

"As I read, I notice that the narrator tells me how Harry looks, acts, and feels. Since the story is meant to entertain us, the narrator includes details that are funny (for example, Harry changed from a white dog with black spots to a black dog with white spots). As a reader, I must count on the narrator to tell me the most important information in this story. I wonder how different the story would be if Harry told it from his point of view?"

> Think about who is telling the story.

Discuss with children how the author entertains readers with the story. Ask them to recall events they liked or thought were funny.

WRITE and APPLY

"If you are ready to work on a new story today, you might consider writing it from the viewpoint of someone who 'watches' the story happen. As you write your story, remember that the reader is counting on you as the narrator to explain how the characters look, act, and feel."

When Harry Met the Scrub Brush

ACTIVITY A

MATERIALS
- *Harry the Dirty Dog* by Gene Zion (HarperCollins)
- chart paper

Reread *Harry the Dirty Dog*. Discuss with children what we learn about Harry from the narrator. Draw three columns on a piece of chart paper. Write *Looks*, *Acts*, and *Feels* at the top of separate columns. Ask children how the narrator describes how Harry looks, acts, and feels, and write their ideas in the corresponding columns. Encourage children to list other things a narrator might reveal about a story, such as where the story takes place.

Looks	Acts	Feels
Has black and white spots	Avoids baths	Sad when he runs away

A Dog's Life

ACTIVITY B

MATERIALS
- *Harry the Dirty Dog* by Gene Zion
- chart paper

Invite children to imagine the story of *Harry the Dirty Dog* from the perspective of one of Harry's family members. Use shared writing to rewrite the story from the perspective of this narrator. Read aloud the story you have written together. Ask children to compare the story written from this point of view with the original. What information would this person know? How would he or she feel?

He rolls in the dirt!

My dog, Harry, is lovable, but he hates to take a bath! Harry gets very dirty and Mom does not like it.

STANDARDS CONNECTION
- Understand that stories can be written from different points of view
- Identify the point of view of a story
- Create a story with a beginning, a middle, and an end

Telling Your Own Story

"We know that a narrative is a story told by a speaker called a **narrator**. Sometimes the narrator, or storyteller, is also the main character of the story. In books like this, main characters tell the reader about their own actions and feelings through their own eyes as they participate in the events of the story."

MATERIALS

- *Alexander and the Terrible, Horrible, No Good, Very Bad Day* by Judith Viorst (Aladdin)

"In the book *Alexander and the Terrible, Horrible, No Good, Very Bad Day*, the author tells the story from the main character's point of view, or through the eyes of Alexander. As you listen to the story, think about the words the author uses to tell us what is happening to Alexander and how it makes him feel. Remember that the author, Judith Viorst, is writing as if she were Alexander, so she will use words like *I*, *me*, and *my*."

Sometimes an author tells a story from his or her own point of view.

Read the first few pages of the book aloud, emphasizing Alexander's response to each event that happens in his day (i.e., 'I could tell it was going to be a terrible, horrible, no good, very bad day' and 'I think I'll move to Australia.')

"I can tell this story is told by Alexander because the words *I*, *me*, and *my* are used to describe his reaction to the event that just took place. Imagine how this story would be different if it were told by a narrator who 'watched' the events taking place. Do you think we would be able to understand what Alexander is feeling as well as we do now? Sometimes an author will choose to tell a story from the main character's point of view so we can see the events through their eyes and better understand what they are feeling."

"Think about some events, either good or bad, that have happened today and how you reacted to them. Record these in your writing folder. Use one of these memories to write from the point of view of the main character the next time you begin a new story."

I Said, He Said, She Said

MATERIALS

• *Alexander and the Terrible, Horrible, No Good, Very Bad Day* by Judith Viorst (Aladdin Books)

Review *Alexander and the Terrible, Horrible, No Good, Very Bad Day.* Write *Point of View* on a piece of chart paper. Divide the chart paper into three columns. Remind children that the main character of the story is also narrating it. Judith Viorst uses the words *I, me,* and *my* to show that it is Alexander who is telling the story. Encourage students to think about the events that happen over the course of Alexander's day (waking up with gum in his hair, finding out he has a cavity, having lima beans for dinner, etc.), and how they caused him to react. Record the event in the first column. In the middle column, have children recall Alexander's response to the event (be sure to use *I, me* or *my* to indicate first-person narration). In the third column, brainstorm with students how the sentence might look if it were written by a narrator who "watching" the story happen. After completing the chart, ask students which version they find more interesting and why.

Point of View		
Alexander has a cavity and the dentist tells him to come back next week.	"Next week," I said, "I'm going to Australia."	Alexander said that he didn't want to come back next week.

From a Pig's Point of View

MATERIALS

• *Pigsty* by Mark Teague (Scholastic)

Read *Pigsty* to the class. Discuss with children that the story is written by a narrator who "watches" the story happen. Review the events of the story with children. Recall that the narrator describes how Wendell, the main character, keeps his room so messy that actual pigs move in because they feel so at home there. Talk about how Wendell enjoys the pigs' company until they start ruining his toys. Finally, Wendell decides to clean his room, and the pigs go back to the farm. Ask children to imagine how the story might be different if it were told from a pig's point of view. Have children help you rewrite *Pigsty* on chart paper from a pig's perspective. Remind children that you will use the words *I, me,* and *my* to tell the story because you are pretending to be the pig.

STANDARDS CONNECTION

✐ Understand that stories can be written from different points of view

✐ Write a story from a certain point of view

✐ Compare points of view

Journals

READ and THINK

"A writer writes in a journal to keep a record of things he or she sees, hears, feels, thinks, or wonders. When people write in a journal or diary, they write the date and then whatever is on their mind. A journal is written from the writer's point of view."

MATERIALS

• *Diary of a Worm* by Doreen Cronin (Joanna Cotler Books)

"Doreen Cronin wrote a story titled *Diary of a Worm* in the form of a journal. In the book, the main character, a worm, writes in a journal about how his friends and family live, learn, and get along with each other. Let's read the story to see how a journal works."

Begin to read aloud the story. "The first thing I notice about this story is that it begins with a date and then some text. The date and text are followed by another date and some more text. One date and the text that follows are called an **entry**."

Continue reading aloud. "The entries in worm's journal help me imagine what it might be like to be a worm. The illustration for each entry matches its text closely and also makes the book more interesting."

WRITE and APPLY

"If you are ready to begin writing a new story, you might consider writing in the form of a diary or a journal. Remember to write the date before each entry."

ACTIVITY A
Diary Style

MATERIALS

- *Diary of a Worm* and *Diary of a Spider* by Doreen Cronin (Joanna Cotler Books)

Review with children that the author of *Diary of a Worm* chose to have her main character tell the story by writing in a journal. Discuss some things we learn about Worm from the author's voice. Tell children that the author wrote another book from the point of view of one of Worm's friends, Spider. Read aloud *Diary of a Spider*. Discuss with children how they can tell that both *Diary of a Spider* and *Diary of a Worm* were written by the same author. Emphasize that there are language patterns and humorous techniques that make up the author's voice that help us recognize her writing.

In both stories, the author has a grandparent teaching little worms or spiders.

ACTIVITY B
Diary of a Young Writer

MATERIALS

- writing booklets (see page 8)

Review with children the purpose and structure of a diary or a journal. Give each child a writing booklet. Invite children to write a journal entry every day that describes the life of a young learner. Have children share their journals after a full week of writing.

$4+1=5$
$6+1=7$
May 15
Today we prctcd adding numbers.

STANDARDS CONNECTION

- Identify the point of view of a story
- Recognize the characteristics of a journal
- Understand that each author has a writing style

Nonfiction

MATERIALS

• *Our Stars*
by Anne Rockwell
(Silver Whistle/
Harcourt Brace)

"Sometimes the stories we read are about things that are real. We call these stories **nonfiction** because they do not come from our imagination. Nonfiction stories are filled with facts about real things."

"Anne Rockwell wrote a book titled *Our Stars* that has information and illustrations about stars and other parts of our solar system. When we read this book, we learn facts about real things."

Read aloud the story. Point out how the illustrations further explain the text. "Sometimes facts are easier to understand when we see a picture of them. I like the close-up picture of the star because it helps me understand that stars are made of fiery gases." Review other information presented in the text and illustrations. Discuss with children that the author's purpose for writing nonfiction is to teach us something new.

"If you are ready to work on something new today, you might like to write a nonfiction story about something you know. Remember to include facts in your nonfiction story, and use illustrations to explain your text."

ACTIVITY A

Celestial Stories

MATERIALS

- *Our Stars* by Anne Rockwell (Silver Whistle/ Harcourt Brace)
- star cutouts
- sentence strip
- glue sticks
- black craft paper

Review with children that *Our Stars* is nonfiction, or a story about something real. Reread the story, and ask children to name facts they learned about stars from the story. Write each fact on a separate star cutout. Write *Facts from Our Stars* by Anne Rockwell on a sentence strip, and glue it to a sheet of black craft paper. Ask children to help you glue the stars to the paper. Display the paper, and encourage children to use the facts to help you write a class story about stars.

ACTIVITY B

Hula Hoop Groups

MATERIALS

- collection of fiction and nonfiction books
- hula hoops
- boxes

Display a collection of fiction and nonfiction books. Discuss the difference between fiction and nonfiction. Arrange two hula hoops side by side on the floor. Read aloud each book title, and ask children whether the book is fiction or nonfiction. Place all fiction books in one hoop and all nonfiction books in the other hoop. Discuss with children the difference in author's purposes between the groups of books. Store each group of books in separate boxes labeled *Fiction* and *Nonfiction*, and encourage children to examine them during silent reading time.

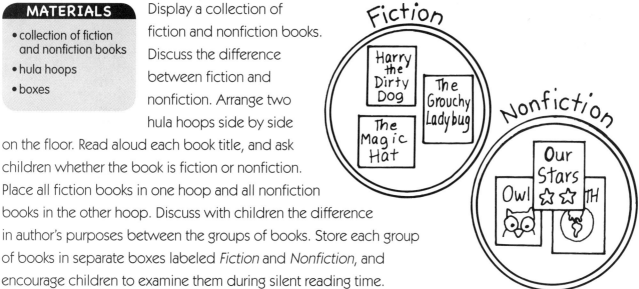

STANDARDS CONNECTION

- ✎ Distinguish fiction from nonfiction text
- ✎ Identify details in nonfiction text
- ✎ Recognize the author's purpose for writing

Let's Write at Home

Dear Family,

Our community of writers has been busy thinking about how to write a good story. We do this by looking at how good writers write. Lately, we have been examining the point of view of an author.

We have learned that a story can be told by different characters (e.g., the main character or a narrator who "watches" a story happen). A story told in the form of entries is called a journal, and writing that is about things that are real is called nonfiction.

This week, try keeping a family journal. Help your child draw or write an entry on each of five consecutive days. Talk about what you would like to record, and remember to write the date above each new entry. Use the attached sheet, A Week in the Life of ___'s Family, as the cover of your journal. Staple five pages behind it. Have your child bring his or her journal to school by _____.

Your child will share the journal with our community of writers. We will talk about why we write in journals and think about ways to make journal writing more interesting.

Sincerely,

Name _____ Date _____
A Week in the Life of
___Sarah___ 's Family

Building a Community of Writers © 2002 Creative Teaching Press

Name _____ Date _____

A Week in the Life of
_____'s Family

Author & Subject Studies

8

When children learn to appreciate an author's style and subject matter, they will become better readers and writers. Present these topics using fun but practical methods.

MINI-LESSON 1   # Lois Ehlert

READ and THINK

"We can learn about good writing when we look closely at the stories of our favorite authors. One of my favorite authors is Lois Ehlert. Lois Ehlert writes and illustrates her stories—just like you do!"

Hmm... What is it that makes this author special?

"I like Lois Ehlert's work because she explains and celebrates nature using colorful language and illustrations. Her artwork is done using a special technique called **collage**. She cuts shapes out of paper and arranges them to make a picture."

"I have collected several examples of Lois Ehlert's work for us to read and study. As we read her books, we will think about what makes Lois Ehlert's text and illustrations unique and special."

MATERIALS

- books by author Lois Ehlert

  Fish Eyes: A Book You Can Count On (Red Wagon Books)

  Growing Vegetable Soup (Red Wagon Books)

  In My World (Harcourt)

  Pie in the Sky (Harcourt)

  Planting a Rainbow (Harcourt)

  Waiting for Wings (Harcourt)

WRITE and APPLY

"Lois Ehlert finds many of her ideas in nature. Look out the window, and write a few of the things you see in your writing folder. Think about using one of these ideas for a story the next time you write."

"READ and THINK" Review

ACTIVITY A

MATERIALS

• *Pie in the Sky* by Lois Ehlert (Harcourt)

Read aloud *Pie in the Sky*. Point out to children that this story is a first-person narrative because a little boy is telling a story from his point of view. Remind children that stories told in the first person use words like *I*, *me*, and *mine*. Explain that this story is unique because there is a second story being told on the bottom corner of each page. Ask children to listen for the repeating line in this story.

> The author uses describing words.

> The author repeats, "But no pie."

Read the story aloud. Ask children where they think Lois Ehlert got her idea for this story. Discuss how the story flows with the seasonal tree changes. Point out the descriptive words that appear in the text in the corner of the pages. Ask children to identify capital letters, periods, question marks, and exclamation points they see.

In Our World

ACTIVITY B

MATERIALS

• *In My World* by Lois Ehlert (Harcourt)
• chart paper
• writing booklets (see page 8)

Read aloud *In My World*. Ask children to name the things the first-person narrator likes (e.g., *creeping bugs, wiggling worms, leaping frogs*). At the top of a piece of chart paper, write *Our world is made up of things we like.*

Invite children to name things they like, and write them on the paper. Remind children to follow the pattern in Lois Ehlert's book (i.e., *ing* adjective and a noun). Give each child a writing booklet, and have children write and illustrate their own list of things they like.

Our world is made up of things we like.

purring cats
shining stars
blooming flowers

STANDARDS CONNECTION

✐ Recognize the characteristics of an author's particular style and voice
✐ Evaluate why an author's work is effective
✐ Recognize patterned structures in text

MINI-LESSON 2

Pat Hutchins

"Pat Hutchins has been writing and illustrating books for a long time, and she has a style all her own. We can hear her voice in her text and identify the technique she uses to draw her illustrations."

"I like Pat Hutchins because she uses rhyme in her text. Although her illustrations are simple, they match her text very well."

"Pat Hutchins is also very good at organizing her work in a sequence. When we read her books, pay attention to the way her ideas are connected in order."

Choose a story or stories from the Materials list to read to your class. All of the recommended books highlight the sequence of events. As you read, emphasize the order of the story and how rhyme is used to achieve this.

MATERIALS

• books by author Pat Hutchins

The Doorbell Rang (Greenwillow Books)

Ten Red Apples (Greenwillow Books)

The Wind Blew (Aladdin)

I like that Pat Hutchins's stories rhyme.

"Think about your favorite Pat Hutchins story and how you can use it as an idea for your own story. Write your idea in your writing folder."

Story Sequencing

ACTIVITY A

MATERIALS

- *The Wind Blew* by Pat Hutchins (Aladdin)
- drawing paper
- crayons or markers
- stapler
- construction paper

Read *The Wind Blew* aloud to the class. Ask children to name in order the objects the wind blew away. Write the name of each object (*umbrella, balloon, hat, kite, shirt, hanky, wig, letters, flag, scarves,* and *newspaper*) along the bottom of separate sheets of papers, and ask children to illustrate the pages. Reread the story, and invite children to line up in the order their object is named in the story. Staple the pages together in order inside a construction paper cover titled *What the Wind Blew*. Place the book at the writing center with a copy of *The Wind Blew*. Encourage children to compare the books and use them to help spell new words in their own writing.

ACTIVITY B

Who Could It Be Now?

MATERIALS

- *The Doorbell Rang* by Pat Hutchins (Greenwillow Books)
- drawing paper
- crayons or markers

Read aloud *The Doorbell Rang*. Discuss with children the patterns (e.g., every time the doorbell rings, more children enter and the kids divide the cookies again), repeating lines (e.g., *as the doorbell rang*), and conventions (i.e., periods, exclamation points, quotation marks) in the story. Give children a piece of paper, and have them draw a picture and write about who they think is at the door at the end of the story.

STANDARDS CONNECTION

- Recognize the characteristics of an author's particular style and voice
- Sequence story events
- Make predictions about what will happen next in a story

Community Workers

READ and THINK

"Many people in our community help us. Let's read some books about them. These books explain in a unique or unusual way the jobs real people do."

MATERIALS

• *I Stink!*
by Kate McMullan
(Joanna Cotler Books)

• *The Jolly Postman*
by Allan Ahlberg
(Little, Brown and Company)

• *Officer Buckle and Gloria*
by Peggy Rathmann
(Putnam)

"This first story, *I Stink!*, is written by Kate McMullan. It is told by a garbage truck!" Read aloud *I Stink!* "This story made me think about garbage trucks in a new way. I knew they were useful, but I never thought about how much work they really do."

On a different day, introduce *The Jolly Postman*. "This story titled *The Jolly Postman* is written by Allan Ahlberg. In this book, the narrator describes how the postman delivers his letters. We also get to read some of these letters, which is like reading a journal." Read aloud *The Jolly Postman*.

"I like this story. I think it is great to be able to read the letters the postman delivers. I like the way the story flows. The writer keeps the story moving by having the postman stop at each house for tea so we can read the letter."

I could write a story about my teacher!

On a different day, introduce *Officer Buckle and Gloria*. "This story by Peggy Rathmann is titled *Officer Buckle and Gloria*. In this story, Officer Buckle is trying very hard to teach children about safety. Let's see how Officer Buckle does." Read aloud *Officer Buckle and Gloria*. "I like this story because it is funny and has a great ending. Officer Buckle does a good job explaining safety tips, but the children find it boring until his dog, Gloria, begins acting them out. I think the author did a good job of showing that this important police officer is just a regular person who has the same feelings as you and me."

WRITE and APPLY

"Think about some of the people in your community who help you. List them in your writing folder. When you are ready to write a new story, consider writing about one of these community helpers."

ACTIVITY A
Talking Tools

MATERIALS
- *I Stink!* by Kate McMullan (Joanna Cotler Books)
- chart paper
- writing booklets (see page 8)

Reread *I Stink!* Discuss with children how the story is written from the garbage truck's point of view. Ask children to think of tools and vehicles other community workers use (e.g., letter carrier's mail truck, baker's rolling pin, teacher's globe, firefighter's fire truck), and write them on chart paper. Choose one object, and write a short class story from that "character's" perspective. Afterward, give each child a writing booklet. Invite children to write a story from the perspective of one of the tools or vehicles on the list. Remind children to use the words *I, me,* and *my.* Encourage children to use descriptive words in their writing. Ask volunteers to share their stories aloud.

> ### I Fight Fires!
> Firemen sound my loud siren and cars move. I take firemen to burning buildings. Sometimes they climb my long ladders to rescue people.

ACTIVITY B
Delivering Thanks to Community Workers

MATERIALS
- stationery
- envelopes
- stamps

Have children brainstorm people in their school community who help them. Invite children to choose a piece of stationery and write a letter to one of the people on the list. Model how to write a letter. Write vocabulary children might use (e.g., *Dear, thank you, helping, sincerely*) on the board. Encourage children to thank the community helpers or ask them questions about their job in their letter. Help children insert their letters in envelopes and then address them. Lead children around the school to deliver their letters.

> Dear Ms. Rae,
> Thnk you for helping me find good books.
> Your friend,
> Jose

STANDARDS CONNECTION
- Identify the point of view of a story
- Write a story from a certain point of view
- Share writing samples aloud

Let's Write at Home

Dear Family,

A great way to help your young writer think about good writing is to look at several titles by a particular author or in a specific subject area. This will help your child compare and contrast different ways to present ideas in writing.

Visit the library and collect a few books by a favorite author or on a favorite subject. Here is a list of authors you and your child might enjoy.

Jim Aylesworth	Laura Numeroff
Lois Ehlert	Audrey Penn
Denise Fleming	Simms Taback
Mary Ann Hoberman	Nancy Tafuri
Pat Hutchins	Iza Trapani
Ezra Jack Keats	Martin Waddell
Jean Marzollo	Nadine Bernard Westcott
Robert Munsch	Jane Yolen

About the Author

Hao was born on June 15 and lives in California with his mom and 2 brothers

The author likes to play soccer and eat pizza

This is a list of things the author likes to write about:
pet snake
bugs
stars

Our next project will be to create an anthology of writing by our favorite authors—the children in our community of writers. Children will choose their favorite piece of writing from their writing portfolio. We will bind a copy of each child's writing together in a book titled *The Best of Our Community of Writers.*

Please help your child complete the About the Author page attached to this sheet. Have your child bring it back to school by _____. We will include this page with your child's writing.

Sincerely,

About the Author

_____

was born on _____

and lives in _____

with _____

_____.

The author likes to _____

_____

This is a list of things the author likes to write about:

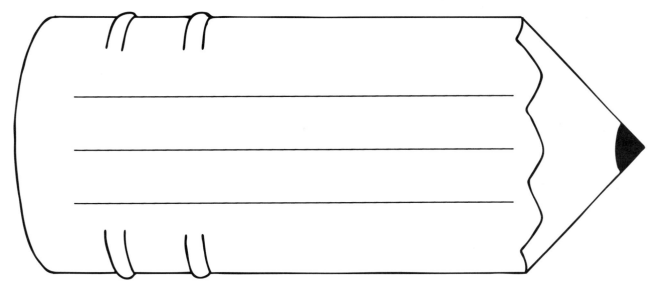

Celebrating Our Community of Writers

Your young writers have spent a productive year examining and practicing the craft of writing. The best way to celebrate the accomplishments of your writing community is to share with children's families. Invite families to school so they can listen to their young authors present their favorite writing.

Copy the end-of-the-year parent letter on page 93, and fill in the missing information. Send a letter home with each child. If you have a large class, you might consider selecting two days to celebrate, and invite half of the families to attend on each day.

Arrange the furniture in your classroom to accommodate the audience, and provide a special place for the authors to wait for their turn to present. Select a suitable chair for the presenting author. Collect children's favorite writing ahead of time, and store it near the author's chair.

Before the presentation, encourage children to select their favorite piece of writing, and have them practice reading it aloud to a classmate. Remind children to use slow, clear voices when reading aloud. Then review with children the behaviors expected of the audience (e.g., no talking while an author reads aloud, clap politely when an author has finished reading).

You may also like to request parent volunteers to provide healthy drinks and snacks for a small reception after the authors have finished their presentations. As children celebrate with their families, congratulate them on a job well done and encourage them to continue reading like writers and writing like readers all summer long!

Dear Parents,

Please join us on _____

at _____ to help us celebrate all that our

community of writers has accomplished this year.

Each of our young writers has selected his or her favorite

piece of writing to read aloud. Our presentation will be

followed by a short reception.

Thank you for your support this year. You have been an

important part of our community of writers, too!

Sincerely,

PERFORMANCE CHECKOFF: **Emergent & Early Writers**

Student's Name _____	Date	Comments
Conveys ideas using pictures or symbols		
Writes from left to right		
Spells words based on initial and ending sounds		
Reads and shares own writing		
Includes some middle sounds when spelling words		
Writes using whole words		
Uses spaces between words		
Writes simple sentences that make sense		
Uses capital letters and periods		
Expands sentences to include three or more elements		
Writes multiple sentences that share a common theme		
Stays focused on the topic		
Writes sentences that include a beginning, a middle, and an end		
Organizes story ideas in logical sequence		

Building a Community of Writers © 2007 Creative Teaching Press

PERFORMANCE CHECKOFF: **Developing & Established Writers**

Student's Name _____	Date	Comments
Includes a title		
Organizes story ideas in logical sequence		
Uses supporting details		
Stays focused on the topic		
Writes sentences and stories that have a clear beginning, middle, and end		
Varies the length of sentences		
Varies the way sentences begin		
Uses literary devices (metaphor/simile)		
Writes in paragraph form		
Writes descriptive stories		
Writes narrative stories		
Writes persuasive stories		
Writes informational passages		
Revises to strengthen content		
Edits for punctuation, grammar, and spelling		

Literature Selections

The literature associated with the mini-lessons in this book have been chosen in part because the text features words that will bolster a child's vocabulary development and inspire expanded word choices. Expose children at all developmental levels to rich language. Children learn new vocabulary when it is explained in context and then experiment with these words in their own writing.

Alexander and the Terrible, Horrible, No Good, Very Bad Day by Judith Viorst

Alligator Baby by Robert Munsch

Bear Wants More by Karma Wilson

Blueberries for Sal by Robert McCloskey

Caps for Sale by Esphyr Slobodkina

Charlie Needs a Cloak by Tomie dePaola

The Crunching Munching Caterpillar by Sheridan Cain

Diary of a Spider by Doreen Cronin

Diary of a Worm by Doreen Cronin

Don't Let the Pigeon Drive the Bus! by Mo Willems

The Doorbell Rang by Pat Hutchins

Down by the Station by Will Hillenbrand

Fall Leaves Fall! by Zoe Hall

Fish Eyes: A Book You Can Count On by Lois Ehlert

Five Little Monkeys Jumping on the Bed by Eileen Christelow

From Head to Toe by Eric Carle

Grandmother Winter by Phyllis Root

The Grouchy Ladybug by Eric Carle

Growing Vegetable Soup by Lois Ehlert

Harry the Dirty Dog by Gene Zion

How Chipmunk Got His Stripes by Joseph Bruchac

How Do Dinosaurs Say Goodnight? by Jane Yolen

I Know a Shy Fellow Who Swallowed a Cello by Barbara S. Garriel

I Like Me! by Nancy Carlson

I Love You by Jean Marzollo

I Stink! by Kate McMullan

If You Give a Mouse a Cookie by Laura Numeroff

In My World by Lois Ehlert

In the Small, Small Pond by Denise Fleming

The Jolly Postman by Allan Ahlberg

Joseph Had a Little Overcoat by Simms Taback

The Kissing Hand by Audrey Penn

The Magic Hat by Mem Fox

Magic Spring by Nami Rhee

The Mouse Who Cried Cat by Rozanne Lanczak Williams

Officer Buckle and Gloria by Peggy Rathmann

Our Stars by Anne Rockwell

Owl Babies by Martin Waddell

Peter's Chair by Ezra Jack Keats

Pie in the Sky by Lois Ehlert

Pigsty by Mark Teague

Planting a Rainbow by Lois Ehlert

Ribbon Rescue by Robert Munsch

The Seven Silly Eaters by Mary Ann Hoberman

Shy Charles by Rosemary Wells

Skip to My Lou by Nadine Bernard Westcott

The Snowy Day by Ezra Jack Keats

A Story, A Story by Gail E. Haley

Ten Red Apples by Pat Hutchins

Toot and Puddle: The New Friend by Holly Hobbie

Waiting for Wings by Lois Ehlert

Wemberly Worried by Kevin Henkes

What the Sun Sees, What the Moon Sees by Nancy Tafuri

When Lightning Comes in a Jar by Patricia Palacco

Why Mosquitoes Buzz in People's Ears: A West African Tale by Verna Aardema

The Wind Blew by Pat Hutchins